The Patriot Act

by Debra A. Miller

LUCENT BOOKS
A part of Gale, Cengage Learning

Detroit • New York • San Francisco • New Haven, Conn • Waterville, Maine • London

© 2007 Gale, a part of Cengage Learning

For more information, contact
Lucent Books
27500 Drake Rd.
Farmington Hills, MI 48331-3535
Or you can visit our Internet site at gale.cengage.com

LIBRARY OF CONGRESS CATALOGING-IN-PUBLICATION DATA

Miller, Debra A.
  The Patriot Act / by Debra A. Miller.
    p. cm. — (Hot topics)
  Includes bibliographical references and index.
  ISBN 978-1-59018-981-8 (hardcover)
  1. United States. Uniting and Strengthening America by Providing Appropriate Tools Required to Intercept and Obstruct Terrorism (USA PATRIOT ACT) Act of 2001—Juvenile literature. 2. Terrorism—United States—Prevention—Juvenile literature. 3. National security—Law and legislation—United States—Juvenile literature. 4. Civil rights—United States—Juvenile literature. 5. War on Terrorism, 2001—Law and legislation—United States—Juvenile literature. I. Title.
  KF9430.Z9M55 2007
  345.73'02—dc22
36242060414071
2007007799

ISBN-10: 1-59018-981-7

Printed in the United States of America
2 3 4 5 6 7 12 11 10 09 08

CONTENTS

FOREWORD

Young people today are bombarded with information. Aside from traditional sources such as newspapers, television, and the radio, they are inundated with a nearly continuous stream of data from electronic media. They send and receive e-mails and instant messages, read and write online "blogs," participate in chat rooms and forums, and surf the Web for hours. This trend is likely to continue. As Patricia Senn Breivik, the dean of university libraries at Wayne State University in Detroit, states, "Information overload will only increase in the future. By 2020, for example, the available body of information is expected to double every 73 days! How will these students find the information they need in this coming tidal wave of information?"

Ironically, this overabundance of information can actually impede efforts to understand complex issues. Whether the topic is abortion, the death penalty, gay rights, or obesity, the deluge of fact and opinion that floods the print and electronic media is overwhelming. The news media report the results of polls and studies that contradict one another. Cable news shows, talk radio programs, and newspaper editorials promote narrow viewpoints and omit facts that challenge their own political biases. The World Wide Web is an electronic minefield where legitimate scholars compete with the postings of ordinary citizens who may or may not be well-informed or capable of reasoned argument. At times, strongly worded testimonials and opinion pieces both in print and electronic media are presented as factual accounts.

Conflicting quotes and statistics can confuse even the most diligent researchers. A good example of this is the question of whether or not the death penalty deters crime. For instance, one study found that murders decreased by nearly one-third when the death penalty was reinstated in New York in 1995. Death penalty supporters cite this finding to support their argument that the existence of the death penalty deters criminals from committing murder. However, another study found that states without the death penalty have murder rates below the national average. This study is cited by opponents of capital punishment, who reject the claim that the death penalty deters murder. Students need context and clear, informed discussion if they are to think critically and make informed decisions.

The Hot Topics series is designed to help young people wade through the glut of fact, opinion, and rhetoric so that they can think critically about controversial issues. Only by reading and thinking critically will they be able to formulate a viewpoint that is not simply the parroted views of others. Each volume of the series focuses on one of today's most pressing social issues and provides a balanced overview of the topic. Carefully crafted narrative, fully documented primary and secondary source quotes, informative sidebars, and study questions all provide excellent starting points for research and discussion. Full-color photographs and charts enhance all volumes in the series. With its many useful features, the Hot Topics series is a valuable resource for young people struggling to understand the pressing issues of the modern era.

INTRODUCTION

A DELICATE BALANCE

The Uniting and Strengthening America by Providing Appropriate Tools Required to Intercept and Obstruct Terrorism Act of 2001, known as the USA PATRIOT Act or simply the Patriot Act, is a massive and wide-ranging law enacted after the September 11, 2001, terrorist attacks on the World Trade Center and the Pentagon by the Islamic terrorist group al Qaeda. It was proposed by President George W. Bush on September 19, 2001, just days after the 9/11 attack and quickly passed by Congress with little debate or opposition. In the crisis atmosphere immediately following 9/11, almost everyone wanted to do everything possible to prevent further attacks. As President Bush said at the time:

> [The Patriot Act] is essential not only to pursuing and punishing terrorists, but also preventing more atrocities in the hands of the evil ones. This government will enforce this law with all the urgency of a nation at war. The elected branches of our government, and both political parties, are united in our resolve to fight and stop and punish those who would do harm to the American people.[1]

Once passed, however, the Patriot Act quickly became a subject of intense scrutiny and controversy. Although much of the new law was not challenged, critics said certain provisions provided for unprecedented government surveillance of U.S. citizens and residents, with almost no judicial oversight. The government's new surveillance powers, for example, authorized federal law enforcement such as the Federal Bureau of Investigation (FBI) to search people's homes and other properties without advance notice to the owner, to monitor e-mails and Internet communications, and to access a wide variety of business, health, financial, and consumer records, as well as other items.

To conduct these searches and surveillance operations, the government was not required to show that the person being targeted had committed a crime or even that the person was involved in terrorism, but only that the information sought was relevant to a government terrorism investigation. The Patriot Act also permitted much of this surveillance to be carried out in secret; it even prohibited persons or businesses affected by certain types of surveillance from ever revealing the fact that they had

The Joint Operations Command Center centralizes security. New surveillance powers allow federal law enforcement agencies to search homes, to monitor e-mail and the Internet, and to access records.

been asked to provide information to the government. Nor did the act allow judicial challenges to most of the government's new powers. In many cases, the Patriot Act allowed the government largely unrestrained powers to conduct terrorism investigations.

Critics claimed these vastly increased police powers threatened long-standing American freedoms guaranteed in the Constitution—such as the rights to free speech, free association, privacy, and due process of law. Civil liberties groups such as the American Civil Liberties Union (ACLU) filed numerous lawsuits challenging the Patriot Act, and several federal courts ruled against the administration, finding parts of the law unconstitutional. The secrecy provisions of the act and government reluctance to reveal information about its actions made oversight of the law difficult, but media reports surfaced to reveal the FBI's heavy-handed and possibly unconstitutional treatment of some citizens and immigrants, particularly Muslims, followers of Islam. As years passed, some members of Congress proposed reforms to the legislation, and a broad opposition movement developed against a number of the act's provisions, especially those authorizing expanded government surveillance. Opponents hoped to rework the Patriot Act in 2005, when certain parts of the law were due to expire.

President Bush and his supporters, meanwhile, celebrated what they believed were the successes of the act and argued that it had helped prevent further terrorist attacks in the years following 9/11. The Department of Justice reported that it obtained 140 guilty pleas or convictions in terrorism investigations conducted under the Patriot Act and that the law helped to disrupt terrorist operations in a number of American cities. The administration insisted that ordinary Americans were not being targeted for government surveillance and that the new police powers in the Patriot Act were vital for fighting the war on terror and keeping America safe.

After a period of congressional review, the Patriot Act was reauthorized in 2006 with some safeguards to protect civil liberties, but opponents say it is still a dangerous law. Since its renewal, civil libertarians have continued to monitor its use by the government, and they claim to have uncovered evidence of more civil rights abuses. The ACLU, for example, has accused the FBI of

President George W. Bush renewed the Patriot Act in 2006.

conducting surveillance of antiwar groups that pose no terrorist threat and whose only sin was to criticize the president's foreign policy decisions. Critics say the Bush administration is using the war on terror as an excuse to expand the powers of the president and executive branch, at the expense of essential democratic freedoms. The public, once solidly behind the government's war on terror and accepting of the Patriot Act's surveillance provisions, also has begun to question their effect on civil liberties.

The debate over the delicate balance between national security and civil liberties thus appears to be far from over. Some commentators fear that 9/11 could mark America's first major step toward a futuristic surveillance society similar to that portrayed in George Orwell's book *1984*—a society in which the government monitors every aspect of its citizens' lives and attempts to control their thoughts. Others feel confident that Americans would never tolerate such overt restrictions on their basic freedoms. The existing Patriot Act powers may ultimately be accepted as part of the cost of keeping America safe from terrorism, but it is also possible that portions may be further curtailed by future legislation to better protect civil liberties that are the foundation of American democracy. The next reckoning on this issue may come in 2009, when a few of the act's surveillance powers are set to expire for the second time.

CHAPTER 1

A RESPONSE
TO TERROR

The Patriot Act was one of the U.S. government's earliest responses to the September 11, 2001, terrorist attacks on the World Trade Center and the Pentagon. Just one week after the 9/11 attacks, President George W. Bush submitted a massive antiterrorism proposal to Congress. Acting in crisis mode because of the terrorist attacks, both houses of Congress quickly passed the legislation virtually without debate. In order to fight terrorism and prevent another terrorist attack, the Patriot Act made sweeping changes to various existing antiterrorism laws and authorized a new level of secret government surveillance within the United States.

A Lack of Debate

The September 11, 2001, terrorist attacks unleashed a tidal wave of fear, shock, and anger across America and within the U.S. government. The hysteria and patriotism that gripped the nation at this time have been compared to the mood created by the Japanese attack on Pearl Harbor during World War II. Although U.S. troops and facilities had sustained numerous terrorist strikes in foreign lands since the 1980s, 9/11 marked the first time in the nation's history that foreign terrorists had successfully mounted a major attack within the United States. Just days after the attack, on September 15, 2001, President Bush declared war on terror, pledging "a comprehensive assault, . . . a broad and sustained campaign to secure our country and eradicate the evil of terrorism."[2] A few days later, the president was more precise, stating: "We will direct every resource at our command—every means of diplomacy, every tool of intelligence, every instrument of law enforcement, every financial influence, and every weapon of war—to the disruption and to the defeat of the global terror network."[3] The war on terror subsequently produced military actions in Afghanistan and Iraq, but it also included a major push by the administration to increase the federal government's police powers and rewrite the nation's laws on police surveillance.

The Patriot Act was established after the September 11, 2001, terrorist attacks.

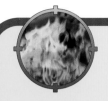

Birth of the Patriot Act

The morning after the 9/11 attacks, a Department of Justice lawyer named Viet Dinh began to plan the government's response to terrorism. Dinh was a thirty-four-year-old native of Vietnam who graduated from Harvard Law School and worked on Capitol Hill for Republican senator Pete Domenici prior to becoming an assistant U.S. attorney at the Justice Department. According to a 2002 *Washington Post* article called "Six Weeks in Autumn," written by Robert O'Harrow Jr., Dinh was instructed by U.S. attorney general John Ashcroft shortly after the 9/11 attacks to prepare a proposal that would include "all that is necessary for law enforcement, within the bounds of the Constitution, . . . to fight this war against terror." Only about a week later, on September 19, 2001, Ashcroft, Dinh, and other Justice Department staff met with congressional and White House leaders in a Senate meeting room to present Dinh's proposal. Democratic senator Patrick Leahy, chair of the Senate Judiciary Committee, also presented a proposal. The two proposals were similar in some ways, but Dinh's version gave the government much broader powers. Dinh's proposal, with very few modifications, was later enacted as the Patriot Act.

Quoted in Robert O'Harrow Jr., "Six Weeks in Autumn," *Washington Post,* October 27, 2002. www.washington post.com/ac2/wp-dyn?pagename=article&contentId =A1999-2002Oct22&notFound=true.

The Bush administration's antiterrorism proposal was sent to Congress on September 19, 2001, only about a week after 9/11. U.S. attorney general John Ashcroft pressured Congress to act quickly, asking legislators to pass the legislation within one week. When this did not happen, Ashcroft complained at an October 1, 2001, press conference that he was "deeply concerned about the rather slow pace [of the legislation]."[4] On October 2, 2001, the administration's proposal was introduced in the House of Representatives by Representative F. James Sensenbrenner, a Republican from Wisconsin. A similar bill was introduced in the Senate on October 4 by Senator Patrick Leahy, a Democrat from Vermont, and the legislation was put on a fast track in both houses.

Indeed, the most notable fact about the Patriot Act was that it produced very little legislative history, because it was enacted quickly with very little debate or time for members of Congress

Members of the House walk out of the Capitol in October 2001 after an anthrax scare.

to evaluate its long-term ramifications. No hearings were held, little time was provided for formal debate, and no experts were called in to evaluate the bill's provisions. Most of the negotiations took place among key congressional leaders and administration officials at informal meetings off-the-record and away from public view. The House Judiciary Committee did spend two weeks considering the bill and making changes to ease members' concerns that some provisions were not constitutional. At the urging of Attorney General Ashcroft, however, House leaders rewrote the bill in the middle of the night to remove these changes and substitute the administration's preferred version of the bill before the full House vote. Most House members who voted on the bill the next day had never even seen it before. There also was no conference committee meeting, a standard procedure in which House and Senate members meet to resolve differences between bills passed by both houses. Instead, House and Senate leaders met informally with administration officials behind closed doors to negotiate the act's final language.

Commentators attribute the legislative rush and the lack of public debate to the highly charged atmosphere that existed in the wake of 9/11. Members of Congress were naturally interested in responding strongly to terrorism, and passing the Patriot Act seemed even more urgent in October 2001 after a series of letters were sent to House and Senate office buildings containing the deadly poison anthrax. It was a time of crisis in which Congress itself seemed under assault, and in which Ashcroft and other Bush administration officials were unrelenting in their pressure for immediate action. Members of Congress worried they would be seen as weak on terrorism if they insisted on taking time to study the administration's proposal or if they voted against it. As John Conyers, the ranking Democrat on the House Judiciary Committee, later explained: "Nearly everybody in both houses voted for the Patriot Act. But they voted for it not knowing what was in it and under a great fear of being considered unpatriotic if they didn't vote for it."[5]

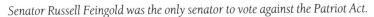

Senator Russell Feingold was the only senator to vote against the Patriot Act.

The abbreviated legislative process and the push for quick passage of the Patriot Act not only cut off congressional review; it also prevented the press, the public, and civil liberties groups from reporting on its provisions or mobilizing any political opposition. As a result, only a few minor changes were made to the final legislation. The most important of these was an agreement for a number of the act's provisions to sunset, or expire automatically, four years later in December 2005. Many members of Congress apparently reasoned that if the law turned out to be flawed, they would have a chance to revisit the issues later. In the end, the legislation was supported by both Republicans and Democrats and was passed by wide margins—in the House by a margin of 357 to 66, and in the Senate by a vote of 98 to 1. Only one senator, Russell Feingold, a Democrat from Wisconsin, voted against it. The Pa-

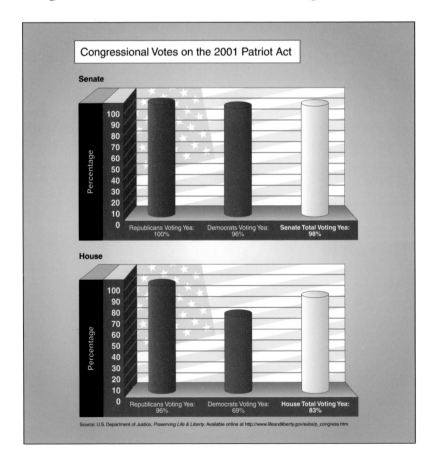

Source: U.S. Department of Justice, *Preserving Life & Liberty.* Available online at http://www.lifeandliberty.gov/subs/p_congress.htm.

triot Act was signed into law by the president on October 26, 2001—just forty-five days after the September 11 attacks.

A Sweeping Law

President Bush, Attorney General Ashcroft, and their supporters argued that the Patriot Act was necessary to give law enforcement the tools necessary to fight terrorism. President Bush said the act would help America "fight the present danger . . . a threat like no other our Nation has ever faced," and he promised that the law "upholds and respects the civil liberties guaranteed by our Constitution."[6] The law's purpose, as described in the act itself, was "to deter and punish terrorist acts in the United States and around the world, to enhance law enforcement investigatory tools, and for other purposes."[7] The Patriot Act was designed to accomplish these goals, in part, by giving police vastly expanded powers to conduct electronic and other surveillance domestically— that is, within the United States. As *Washington Post* reporter Robert O'Harrow Jr. explained:

> The White House, the Justice Department and their allies in Congress wanted to ease . . . restrictions [on electronic eavesdropping and domestic spying that they said] were partly to blame for the intelligence gaps on September 11. . . . The administration also wanted new authority to secretly detain individuals suspected of terrorism and to enlist banks and other financial services companies in the search for terrorist financing. What's more, law enforcement sought broad access to business databases filled with information about the lives of ordinary citizens. All this detail could help investigators search for links among plotters.[8]

Although intended to be used only against suspected terrorists, the broad scope of the Patriot Act would give the government access to a wide range of very detailed information about American citizens. As author Herbert N. Foerstel has described, the government wanted "unfettered access to telephone records, email, library records, and the ocean of data assembled by corporations each day about individuals' personal lives, all to assist in the hunt for potential terrorists."[9]

President George W. Bush signed the Patriot Act into law on October 26, 2001.

To accomplish the administration's goals, the Patriot Act made sweeping changes to numerous federal laws, including some laws that were originally passed to restrict the government's ability to conduct domestic spying and surveillance. One important law affected by the Patriot Act, for example, was the Foreign Intelligence Surveillance Act (FISA), a reform passed in 1978 to correct past surveillance abuses by the FBI, the Central Intelligence Agency (CIA), and other government agencies. These abuses were uncovered in an investigation led by Senator Frank Church in the mid-1970s following Watergate, a scandal that revealed then-president Richard M. Nixon's efforts to conduct secret surveillance of his political enemies. The Church investigation found that the federal government had routinely spied for years on politicians, religious organizations, women's rights advocates, antiwar groups, and civil liberties activists. Some of the worst abuses uncovered were in an FBI program known as COINTELPRO, which was designed to undermine civil rights groups and other political activists. Among other operations, COINTELPRO tried to get targeted individuals fired from their jobs, sent anonymous letters to their spouses in an effort to destroy their marriages, and conducted a sustained campaign to discredit civil rights leader Martin Luther King Jr. by leaking information about his personal life.

FISA was enacted by Congress to prevent this type of secret government spying on U.S. citizens. The law struck a balance: It gave intelligence officials broad powers to monitor spies and the agents of foreign countries but firmly restricted the use of these powers for domestic criminal investigations and prosecutions. Under FISA, investigators were required to clear their surveillance activities by demonstrating that the principal purpose of the surveillance was to obtain foreign intelligence information. The body set up to regulate these surveillance activities was a new, secret court known as the Foreign Intelligence Surveillance Court. Civil libertarians considered FISA one of the main safeguards against domestic spying, but the Patriot Act weakened this safeguard, largely by easing the FISA requirement that foreign intelligence be the main purpose for government spying.

The Patriot Act also modified Title III of the Omnibus Crime Control and Safe Streets Act, a law that set the rules for the government's use of electronic eavesdropping, often called wiretapping. Title III prohibited police eavesdropping on

In the mid-1970s, Senator Frank Church uncovered surveillance abuses by the FBI, CIA, and other government agencies. This led to the Foreign Intelligence Surveillance Act of 1978, which was affected by the Patriot Act.

telephone conversations, face-to-face conversations, or computer and other forms of electronic communications in most cases. It allowed police surveillance only for certain defined offenses, only if certain guidelines were followed, and only if authorized by a court. Title III also set the rules for the use of so-called trap and trace devices and pen registers—instruments that identify the source and destination of calls made to and from a particular telephone, but not the content of those calls. The Patriot Act weakened these restrictions and made it much easier for police to conduct surveillance of all types of electronic communications, including e-mails.

NO DEBATE, NO OPPOSITION

"The [Bush] administration voiced barely veiled threats that anyone who questioned the legislation would be deemed unpatriotic and accused of aiding the terrorists. . . . Not surprisingly, the act sailed through Congress with no hearings, no debate, no deliberation, and almost no opposition."

—Geoffrey R. Stone, law professor at the University of Chicago

Quoted in *Legal Affairs,* "What's Wrong with the Patriot Act?" October 3, 2005. www.legalaffairs.org/webexclusive/debateclub_patact1005.msp.

Expansion of Earlier Antiterrorism Law

Many commentators saw the Patriot Act as the culmination of a pre-9/11 effort by the federal government to expand police and intelligence powers in the name of terrorism. As constitutional scholar David Cole and civil libertarian James X. Dempsey explained, many of the Patriot Act's provisions "were developed long before the bombings that triggered their final enactment."[10] This push for antiterrorist powers was begun by President Ronald Reagan, but his proposals were rejected by Congress on constitutional grounds. The next president, George H.W. Bush, made similar proposals that were again rejected by lawmakers on two separate occasions.

Following the 1993 terrorist bombings of the World Trade Center and the 1995 bombing of the Oklahoma City federal building by homegrown terrorist Timothy McVeigh, however, President Bill Clinton finally convinced Congress in 1996 to enact many of the Reagan and Bush concepts in the Antiterrorism and Effective Death Penalty Act. The act created a special court to hear secret evidence that could be used to deport foreigners labeled as terrorists, made it a crime to give material support (initially interpreted as providing personnel or training) to lawful humanitarian and political activities of organizations labeled as terrorist groups by the U.S. Department of State, and allowed the FBI to investigate anyone who associated with persons suspected as terrorists.

In the years before 9/11, critics argued that many of the provisions of the Antiterrorism Act dangerously weakened civil liberties protected by the Constitution. Terrorism, they said, was becoming the new justification for surveillance abuses. Civil libertarian groups lobbied Congress to repeal parts of the 1996 law, while law enforcement supporters sought even broader powers. The terrorist attacks of 9/11 finally created support for these

The Antiterrorism and Effective Death Penalty Act was enacted in 1996 after a terrorist bombing of the World Trade Center in 1993.

stronger police powers. The Antiterrorism Act thus served as the foundation for the even more expansive antiterrorism powers enacted in the Patriot Act.

Searches and Wiretaps Under Title II

The final version of the 2001 Patriot Act was a huge, 342-page law that was divided into ten titles: Title I—Enhancing Domestic Security Against Terrorism; Title II—Enhanced Surveillance Procedures; Title III—International Money Laundering Abatement and Anti-Terrorism Financing Act of 2001; Title IV—Protecting the Border; Title V—Removing Obstacles to Investigating Terrorism; Title VI—Providing for Victims of Terrorism, Public Safety Officers, and Their Families; Title VII—Increased Information Sharing for Critical Infrastructure Protection; Title VIII—Strengthening the Criminal Laws Against Terrorism; Title IX—Improved Surveillance; and Title X—Miscellaneous. Many of the provisions in these titles attracted little public notice or criticism, but a few became quite prominent in the news.

A TOOL FOR COMBATING TERRORISM

"[The Patriot Act] tools have been indispensable in helping law enforcement protect Americans from further terrorist acts while preserving the liberties that the Constitution guarantees each of us."
—Kevin V. Ryan, former judge on the San Francisco Superior Court and U.S. attorney for the northern district of California since July 2002

Kevin V. Ryan, "Why All Provisions of the Patriot Act Should Be Reauthorized," *San Francisco Chronicle,* May 9, 2005. www.sfgate.com/cgi-bin/article.cgi?file=/chronicle/archive/2005/05/09/EDGM7C904A1.DTL.

Some of the most discussed sections of the act were the new surveillance laws found mostly in Title II. Section 213, for example, authorized law enforcement officers to secretly search citizens' homes or other premises without prior notification to the owner or occupant—a technique often called a sneak-and-peek search. This provision was applied not only to terrorism cases, but to any federal crime. In addition, courts were authorized to permit investigators to seize physical property found in the secret searches in most cases. In the past, law enforcement often had difficulty convincing judges to issue warrants for these types of searches, and if authorized, the police were more closely restricted in their ability to seize evidence found during the searches.

Several other Title II sections expanded the authority of courts to order surveillance of electronic communications. Section 206, for example, provided the FISA court with roving wiretap authority—that is, the ability to authorize investigators to intercept all electronic communications that a targeted suspect might use without specifying the particular telephone line or facility to be monitored. Previous law required authorities to ascertain that a suspect was actually using a particular device, and then required each telephone company or other communication provider to be specified in the court's order. Under the new law, for example, the FBI could monitor all pay phone, cell phone, and Internet communications a suspected terrorist might use in a particular neighborhood or nationwide using one broadly written court order. Another provision, Section 218, changed the standard of proof for FISA surveillance; instead of demonstrating that the purpose of surveillance was to gather foreign intelligence, investigators now needed to show only that foreign intelligence was a "significant purpose" of the search—a much lower legal standard.

Section 214, meanwhile, lowered the standard for pen/trap surveillance (recording the numbers called from a particular telephone) in FISA investigations. Investigators no longer had to show that the

The Patriot Act allows the FBI to monitor all pay phone, cell phone, and Internet activities.

communications to be monitored were those of a suspected foreign spy; Section 214 allowed anyone's communications to be monitored, as long as the surveillance was for a terrorism investigation. Section 216, meanwhile, expanded the reach of pen/trap surveillance to include e-mails and Internet communications—a significantly wider application that provided police with much more information.

Perhaps the most widely debated provision of the Patriot Act, however, was Section 215. It allowed federal investigators to search for "any tangible thing"—a very broad term that could include books, computer records and hard drives, written records, and virtually any other physical object. Section 215 orders had to be approved by a FISA court, but only the government was represented at the court hearing, so no one was present to argue against the search requests. Moreover, the businesses, entities, or persons

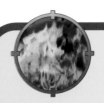

The Secret FISA Court

The Foreign Intelligence Surveillance Act (FISA) was enacted in 1978 to provide rules for when the government can conduct electronic surveillance and physical searches of persons suspected of being foreign spies against the United States. Under the act, federal law enforcement agents from the Department of Justice or U.S. intelligence agencies wishing to conduct wiretaps or searches inside the United States must get the approval of a special eleven-member federal court called the Foreign Intelligence Surveillance Court (FISC or FISA court). The court, located in Washington, D.C., meets in a windowless courtroom in complete secrecy, and its rulings are permanently sealed and never made available to the public. Even Congress is given almost no information about the FISA court's operation; FISA requires only that Congress be provided with the number of surveillance orders approved each calendar year and brief, semiannual reports. During its twenty-five-year-plus existence, the court has handled more than ten thousand requests, but it has only rejected four government applications for search warrants. Although once limited to approving searches for foreign spies, the FISA court's jurisdiction was expanded by the Patriot Act to cover terrorist investigations.

served with Section 215 orders were gagged, or prohibited from disclosing the fact that their records were being searched to anyone else, including the targets of the search. This provision thus allowed the government secretly to keep track of a person's reading, computer, health, spending, or other habits, without ever notifying the person that his or her privacy had been violated.

Together, all of these Title II provisions made it much easier for police to search the property of both U.S. citizens and noncitizens, obtain their personal records, and monitor their communications—secretly and without acquiring a traditional search warrant.

National Security Letters

Section 505 of Title V of the Patriot Act did not receive quite as much publicity as Title II, but it created what many commentators suggested was an even broader expansion of police power—a secret FBI warrant called a National Security Letter (NSL). Prior to the Patriot Act, NSLs were authorized only for certain types of information—telephone and other electronic records under the Electronic Communications Privacy Act, and bank and financial information under the Right to Financial Privacy Act and the Fair Credit Reporting Act. The Patriot Act, however, made it much easier for the FBI to obtain a wider range of electronic and other business records.

Most notably, unlike Section 215, Section 505 allowed the FBI to issue NSLs directly, without asking for any type of court approval, not even from the secret FISA court. In fact, local FBI offices could issue these NSLs without approval from FBI headquarters. In addition, the Patriot Act did not require that investigators show that the records or information sought related to a foreign power or its agents, or even that the person being investigated was involved in terrorist activities. Rather, Section 505 merely required that the information be "sought for the conduct of an authorized investigation to protect against international terrorism or clandestine intelligence activities"[11]—a very low standard.

Also, like Section 215, Section 505 contained a permanent gag order that prevented targets of the NSL from ever disclosing that they received the letter. The Patriot Act provided no process for recipients to petition for the gag order to be lifted, and no judicial or other way to challenge the validity of the NSL. Under Section 505, the government thus had the ability to issue its own search warrants without any form of judicial oversight.

Other Significant Provisions

The Patriot Act made a number of other significant changes or additions to federal law, most of which received less publicity than the Title II and NSL provisions. Section 802, for example, created a new category of crime called domestic terrorism. This crime was defined broadly in the act as "acts dangerous to human life that are a violation of the criminal laws of the United States" if the intent was to "influence the policy of a government by intimidation or coercion." Another provision, Section 805, extended the 1996 ban on providing material support to terrorist organizations by defining it to include not only personnel and training, but also "expert advice or assistance."[12]

Sections 411 and 412, meanwhile, gave federal authorities greater power to detain and deport noncitizens than ever before. Section 411 allowed the secretary of state to designate domestic groups as terrorist organizations and made aliens deportable for associating, even unknowingly, with any group that has been named as a terrorist group. Section 412 provided for the mandatory detention of immigrants suspected of terrorism, allowing them to be held for seven days without charge, based only on the government's certification that there were "reasonable grounds to believe"[13] the person endangered national security.

A few other provisions also attracted media attention. Various Title III sections created a process for the government to quickly and easily acquire financial information from banks and other financial institutions, and Section 508 gave the government access to educational records, all without a court order.

Sunset Provisions

Most of the Patriot Act's provisions made permanent changes in the nation's antiterrorism laws. Under a compromise reluctantly agreed to by the administration, however, Section 224 of the Patriot Act provided that some surveillance provisions would sunset, or automatically expire, on December 31, 2005. The provisions subject to

Section 411 allows the deportation of aliens who associate with known terrorist groups.

sunset included several Title II sections, such as the roving wiretap and records search provisions in Sections 206 and 215, but the sunset law specifically exempted the sneak-and-peek searches in Section 213, the electronic surveillance authorized by Section 216, as well as Sections 203(a), 203(c), 205, 208, 210, 211, 219, 221, and 222. The NSL provision in Section 505 and many other provisions in the act were also permanently authorized. In numerous ways, therefore, the Patriot Act permanently enlarged the government's police powers, all in the name of fighting terrorism.

CHAPTER 2

A CONTROVERSIAL LAW

Almost as soon as it was passed, the Patriot Act became the topic of heated debate as critics around the country claimed that many of its provisions were unconstitutional infringements on Americans' civil liberties. The opposition came from all directions —traditional civil rights advocates such as the American Civil Liberties Union (ACLU), as well as libraries and library associations, state and local governments, and some members of Congress. The resistance took various forms—everything from largely symbolic resolutions to court challenges and proposals for legislative restrictions. As years passed without another terrorist attack, the general public's strong support for the Patriot Act began to be tempered by concerns about civil liberties.

Opposition from Libraries

Some of the earliest opponents to the 2001 Patriot Act were the national American Library Association (ALA) and a variety of state and local library organizations. These groups argued that parts of the act undermined the library community's traditional values of privacy and freedom of access to information. Library patrons, they said, would no longer feel free to use library resources for fear that the government might be monitoring what they were reading or researching. The ALA produced a number of documents analyzing the effects of the Patriot Act on libraries, expressing its opposition to the act's threats to civil liberties, and directing libraries on how best to protect the privacy of library users and respond to government's requests for information under the act. In January 2002, for example, the ALA passed a resolution that reaffirmed the principle of intellectual freedom and encouraged "libraries and their staff to protect the privacy and confidentiality of the people's lawful use of the library, its equipment, and its resources."[14] In 2003, the ALA adopted a resolution calling on Congress to monitor the act's impact and change portions of the law that threaten privacy, free speech, and other constitutional rights. The resolution stated, in part:

> Certain provisions of the USA PATRIOT Act . . . expand the authority of the federal government to investigate citizens and non-citizens, to engage in surveillance, and to threaten civil rights and liberties guaranteed under the United States Constitution and Bill of Rights; . . . therefore, be it RESOLVED, that the American Library Association . . . urges the United States Congress to:
>
> 1) provide active oversight of the implementation of the USA PATRIOT Act and other related measures, and the revised Attorney General Guidelines to the Federal Bureau of Investigation;
>
> 2) hold hearings to determine the extent of the surveillance on library users and their communities; and
>
> 3) amend or change the sections of these laws and the guidelines that threaten or abridge the rights of inquiry and free expression.[15]

A number of state and local library associations also actively joined in the resistance effort.

Librarians were particularly incensed about Sections 214, 215, and 216, which awarded federal investigators broad powers to obtain information about the Internet and book-reading habits of library users. As library advocate Herbert N. Foerstel warned, "Since virtually all libraries now

Janet Nocek, director of the Portland Library in Portland, Connecticut, speaks out against Patriot Act demands for library records.

A button displays a librarian's feelings about certain aspects of the Patriot Act that give the government access to library records.

provide public Internet terminals, they will become targets of these new surveillance powers and will be required to cooperate in the monitoring of a user's electronic communications sent through the library's computers."[16] Foerstel also said that Section 215's "any tangible thing" language is very broad and "allows the FBI to compel the library or bookstore to release virtually any personal information it has maintained, including Internet records and registration information stored in any medium."[17]

In addition, libraries were outraged that they could be the targets of secret, FBI-issued NSLs that prohibited librarians from informing library patrons or colleagues that library resources or records were the object of a federal investigation. Library associations predicted that the FBI would now use NSLs during very preliminary inquiries about terrorism, since NSLs could be issued under the Patriot Act without any type of judicial approval or supervision.

Librarians' concerns were heightened by the results of a survey of more than one thousand libraries conducted by the Library Research Center at the University of Illinois in December 2001, just two months after the passage of the Patriot Act. Among other questions, the survey asked whether law enforcement authorities such as the FBI or the police had requested any information about library patrons relating to the terrorist attacks of September 11.

The responses showed that 11.2 percent of the largest libraries had already been contacted by law enforcement. A similar 2002 study by the Library Research Center found that eighty-five out of about one thousand libraries had been contacted by law enforcement seeking information about patron reading habits. These results garnered national attention, but the numbers were not completely reliable, because they did not differentiate between informal visits, Section 215 orders, and NSL requests, and because the gag provisions of the Patriot Act may have affected the responses. Library advocates pushed for the government to reveal more detailed information about how it was using the Patriot Act in libraries.

IGNORING THE RULE OF LAW

"Sept. 11 does not justify ignoring the Constitution by creating broad new federal police powers. The rule of law is worthless if we ignore it whenever crises occur."

—Ron Paul, Republican representative from Texas

Ron Paul, "Question the PATRIOT Act Now—Before It's Too Late," Antiwar.com, December 27, 2005. www.antiwar.com/paul/?articleid=8310.

State and Local Resistance

In the years after enactment of the Patriot Act, numerous states, cities, and counties also condemned the new law. By the fall of 2005, a total of eight states (Alaska, California, Colorado, Hawaii, Idaho, Maine, Montana, and Vermont) and almost four hundred cities and counties had passed resolutions denouncing the act as an assault on civil liberties. Among the local communities objecting to the law were some of the country's largest cities, including New York City, Los Angeles, Dallas, Chicago, and Philadelphia. A small town in northern California, Arcata, even passed an ordinance outlawing voluntary compliance with the Patriot Act. David Meserve, the freshman City Council member who drafted the ordinance, explained, "It's our citywide form of nonviolent disobedience."[18] A group called the Bill of Rights Defense Committee (BORDC) was formed in 2001 to help coordinate these local anti–Patriot Act efforts.

The SAFE Act

The Security and Freedom Ensured Act (SAFE), also called the Security and Freedom Enhancement Act, has been introduced in both houses of Congress every year since 2003. Its purpose is to safeguard civil liberties by placing a number of limitations on the Patriot Act's search and surveillance powers. Specifically, among other changes, the SAFE Act would limit the use of roving wiretaps by requiring the government to identify the targeted person or location; limit secret sneak-and-peek searches by limiting such searches to situations where notice would endanger life or limb, cause suspects to flee, or result in the destruction of evidence; protect Americans' personal information from searches by requiring that the government show specific facts demonstrating a targeted person is a spy or a terrorist; and prevent the government from searching library records without judicial approval. The act also would impose stricter reporting requirements and eliminate completely several Patriot Act sections, such as Sections 213, 216, and 505. Civil liberties groups continue to urge passage of the SAFE Act as a way to reform the reauthorized Patriot Act.

Many commentators dismissed the resolutions and ordinances as merely symbolic, noting that under the Constitution, federal laws such as the Patriot Act override state and local laws. Others, however, said the widespread opposition helped send a message to federal authorities and legislators that civil liberties must be protected. As Nancy Talanian, BORDC's director, noted, "Such a large, powerful, and nonpartisan groundswell of people acting locally to hold their federal elected representatives accountable is unparalleled in U.S. history."[19] In addition, some experts believe that localities have a legal right to challenge what they view as unconstitutional requirements and to refuse to use local police to enforce the Patriot Act. As David Kopel, a civil liberties expert with the conservative Independence Institute, explained, "Your city couldn't pass a law saying that the Patriot Act does not apply within its city boundaries, but the city can choose not to assist in the enforcement of that law."[20]

Court Challenges

Still further opposition came in the form of lawsuits challenging the constitutionality of various sections of the Patriot Act. In 2003, the ACLU filed the first such lawsuit. The case, called *Muslim Community Association of Ann Arbor et al. v. John Ashcroft*, involved Section 215, which authorized the FBI to obtain tangible things belonging to people without a showing of probable cause that they had engaged in a crime. On behalf of six mostly Muslim American and Arab organizations, the ACLU claimed the statute chilled—that is, discouraged—the exercise of constitutional rights such as the right to freedom of speech, religion, and association. To support this claim, the Muslim Community Association stated in an affidavit that attendance at prayer services and other events had dropped since 9/11 and that donations to the group had dropped by half. Today, the case is still pending in federal district court in Michigan.

A second ACLU lawsuit against the Patriot Act was more successful. The ACLU brought the case, called *Doe and ACLU v. Ashcroft et al.*, on behalf of an Internet service provider that had received a National Security Letter (NSL) from the FBI demanding customer records under Section 505. On September 29, 2004, U.S. district judge Victor Marrero struck down Section 505, ruling that the NSL process chilled First Amendment free speech and that the lack of warrant or any form of meaningful judicial review in Section 505 violated the Fourth Amendment's prohibition against searches without a judicial warrant. The court also found the broad gag provision in the law, which prohibited targets of NSLs from revealing to anyone that they were under investigation, to be an unconstitutional prior restraint on free speech. The ruling was the first court decision to strike down any of the expanded surveillance powers authorized by the Patriot Act, and it was lauded by civil rights advocates as a victory against unchecked government spying. As ACLU executive director Anthony D. Romero explained, "This is a landmark victory against the . . . Justice Department's misguided attempt to intrude into the lives of innocent Americans in the name of national security."[21]

Demonstrators protest the Patriot Act.

Another lawsuit filed by the Humanitarian Law Project (HLP), a nonprofit human rights group, challenged the constitutionality of Section 805 of the Patriot Act. The lawsuit was filed on behalf of five organizations and two U.S. citizens who wanted to provide expert advice to Kurdish refugees in Turkey who were fighting oppression by the Turkish government. HLP challenged a portion of Section 805 that prohibited providing expert advice or assistance to groups designated by the government as foreign terrorist organizations. On January 23, 2004, U.S. district judge Audrey Collins upheld HLP's claim and ruled that Section 805 violated the First and Fifth Amendments to the Constitution because it was so vague that it "could be construed to include unequivocally pure speech and advocacy protected by the First Amendment."[22] Constitutional expert David Cole, who represented HLP in the case, explained the court's ruling:

> This decision calls into question the government's reliance on overbroad laws imposing guilt by association in the war on terrorism. Our clients sought only to support lawful and nonviolent activity, yet the Patriot Act provision draws no distinction whatsoever between expert advice in human

rights, designed to deter violence, and expert advice on how to build a bomb. We think the Constitution demands that the law recognize the difference between furthering human rights and furthering violence.[23]

Nancy Chang, an attorney from the Center for Constitutional Rights and cocounsel on the case, also applauded the ruling. She stated: "The Patriot Act was passed by Congress in tremendous haste and with little deliberation over its restrictions on civil liberties, under intense pressure from the Bush administration. The court's ruling affirms the principle that, in fighting terrorism, Congress and the President are not free to ignore our fundamental constitutional rights."[24]

The ACLU also launched a $3.5 million campaign against the Patriot Act. Part of the campaign was a print advertisement run in magazines in 2003 that criticized the act's assault on civil liberties and urged Americans to act before their freedoms disappeared. The ad read:

> Today, the government can get a secret warrant to search your home without telling you until long afterwards. . . . Today, the government can monitor your Internet use, read your emails, examine your online purchases with minimal judicial oversight. Today, you can be detained without access to a lawyer, without being charged with a crime. Today, [Attorney General] John Ashcroft has authorized the FBI to monitor your political activities, to send agents into your house of worship. We can only guess what tomorrow will bring."[25]

The ACLU launched a campaign against the Patriot Act criticizing Attorney General John Ashcroft's authorization of expanded police powers for the FBI.

Congressional and Public Oversight

Given the expedited passage of the Patriot Act and the rising concerns about civil liberties, many members of Congress realized the importance of vigilant congressional oversight of the law. Legislative attempts to monitor the act, however, were made extremely difficult by Bush administration officials who repeatedly refused to release information to Congress. As Herbert N. Foerstel reports, "During the first ten months after the passage of the Patriot Act, the Senate Judiciary Committee [which has oversight authority over the Patriot Act] sent twenty-seven unanswered letters to the Justice Department seeking information on the Patriot Act and related matters."[26] Senator Patrick Leahy, chairman of the Judiciary Committee, commented, "Since I've been here, I have never known an administration that is more difficult to get information from that the oversight committees are entitled to."[27] The House of Representatives experienced the same problems getting information about implementation of the act.

The questions asked by Congress concerned issues such as what tangible things the government had sought in investigations of U.S. citizens under Section 215, the scope of the department's use of NSLs, and the guidelines being used for requiring businesses to hand over electronic records on finances, telephone calls, e-mails, and other personal data. The government claimed that much of this data was classified and could not be revealed. "Classified" was the response, for example, even to congressional questions about the total numbers of FBI Section 215, NSL, or wiretap requests.

In May 2003, the Justice Department finally produced a sixty-page report and allowed Assistant Attorney General Viet Dinh, the main author of the administration's Patriot Act proposal, to testify before the Senate Judiciary Committee. Although still withholding specific data that it said was highly classified, the report stated that federal agents had conducted hundreds of secret searches and surveillance operations and visited numerous libraries and mosques, and that some fifty people had been detained without charges as material witnesses. Attorney General Ashcroft, the report said, had approved 113 emergency authorizations for secret warrants for electronic or physical evidence, more than double the number used in the previous twenty-three years. Moreover, Assistant Attorney General Viet Dinh testified, "[A]gents have contacted about 50 libraries nationwide in the course of terrorism investigations, often at the invitation of librarians who saw something suspicious."[28]

LOSS OF LIBERTY IS UNTRUE

"To those who scare peace-loving people with phantoms of lost liberty, my message is this: Your tactics only aid terrorists—for they erode our national unity and diminish our resolve."
—John Ashcroft, U.S. attorney general from 2001 to 2004

Quoted in Nancy V. Baker, "National Security Versus Civil Liberties," *Presidential Studies Quarterly*, September 2003, p. 547.

Frustrated by Congress's inability to shed light on the specifics of the Patriot Act's implementation, several public advocacy groups pursued another tactic, submitting a Freedom of Information Act request to the government in August 2002. Most of the information sought in the request was denied by the Department of Justice, but the department did produce two hundred pages of heavily edited documents that included five pages of logs of NSL requests between October 2001 and January 2003. Although much of the information was blacked out, civil liberties advocates said the size of the logs showed that NSLs had already become a popular FBI surveillance tool, no doubt because they required no judicial approval. Unsatisfied with this partial response, the ACLU and other organizations filed suit to force the federal government to release statistical information detailing the government's use of the Patriot Act. On May 19, 2003, however, in *ACLU v. Department of Justice*, the District Court of the District of Columbia rejected the claim and ruled that the information could be withheld on national security grounds. Critics said the court's decision meant that the administration was successful in preventing both Congress and the public from closely monitoring how the government's use of the Patriot Act was affecting citizens' privacy and other constitutional rights.

Legislative Efforts to Limit the Patriot Act

Beginning in 2003, several members of Congress began introducing legislation to correct what they viewed as defects of the Patriot Act. In the House of Representatives, for example, Representative Bernie Sanders (an Independent from Vermont) introduced the Freedom to Read Act (HR 1157), which sought to limit the use of FISA orders to get libraries' or booksellers' patron records. The legislation had seventy-three cosponsors, demonstrating its wide appeal. In addition, Representative Dennis Kucinich (a Democrat from Ohio) introduced the Benjamin Franklin True Patriot Act (HR 3171) to require a review of antiterrorism legislation to ensure that it does not inappropriately undermine civil liberties.

As in the House, Senate attempts to curtail the Patriot Act focused on limiting the government's access to library and

Senator Patrick Leahy, left, and Representative Bernie Sanders attend the Vermont Democratic Party election in 2004. Sanders introduced the Freedom to Read Act to try and correct some of the aspects of the Patriot Act.

Homeland Security Act

The Homeland Security Act was introduced soon after the passage of the Patriot Act and enacted in November of 2002. The act reorganized the federal government and created a new federal Department of Homeland Security (DHS) to oversee twenty existing federal agencies —the biggest change in government in fifty years. The purpose of the act was to encourage federal agencies to work more closely with each other in the fight against terrorism, and it granted Patriot Act–like powers to many of these federal agencies. Civil liberties groups objected strongly to the act, claiming it reduced privacy, increased government surveillance powers, and promoted government secrecy. One of the most controversial parts of the act was a Pentagon project called Total Information Awareness (TIA). Critics warned that the project would create computer files on every American by monitoring consumer transactions, finances, education, medical history, travel, personal communications, and public records. The Senate cut funding for TIA in 2003, but legislators allowed the government to continue secretly using some data-mining technologies, as long as they are not used on Americans within the United States. Civil liberties groups, however, continue to criticize the act.

bookstore records. Bills in this category included the Booksellers and Personal Records Privacy Act (S 1507), introduced by Senator Russell Feingold, and the Library and Bookseller Protection Act (S 1158), introduced by Senator Barbara Boxer. Two other Senate efforts included the PATRIOT Oversight and Restoration Act (S 1695), a bill introduced by Senator Patrick Leahy to add to the list of Patriot Act sections due to expire at the end of 2005, and the Protecting the Rights of Individuals Act (S 1552), legislation introduced by Senator Lisa Murkowsky to amend the federal criminal code and FISA to strengthen civil liberties protections.

Only one piece of legislation was introduced in both the House and the Senate—the Security and Freedom Ensured (SAFE) Act (HR 3352, S 1709, and S 737). It was introduced in the House by Representative C.L. Otter and in the Senate by

Senator Larry Craig—both Republicans from Idaho. If passed, the SAFE Act would have limited not only FISA orders to libraries and booksellers, but also the use of sneak-and-peek searches and roving wiretaps. In addition, it would have changed several other Patriot Act provisions and increased the government's reporting requirements. This legislation was strongly opposed by the administration; in January 2004, Attorney General Ashcroft sent a letter to the Senate Judiciary Committee arguing that the act would "undermine our ongoing campaign to detect and prevent catastrophic terrorist attacks"[29] and threatening a Bush administration veto.

None of these bills was ever passed; instead, they were simply referred to committees, where no hearings were held and they languished for lack of support. The House did pass amendments to appropriations legislation to cut off funding to the Department of Justice for Section 213 sneak-and-peek searches and for Section 215 records searches, but the Senate did not agree. Even if these limits on appropriations had been enacted by Congress, however, experts said they would have been largely symbolic, since the Department could still use NSLs instead of Section 215 to acquire records, and since it could probably manipulate its budget to continue to fund Section 215 searches.

Public Opinion

Despite the opposition of libraries and civil rights groups, during the first couple of years following 9/11, public opinion appeared to support the Patriot Act. An aura of fear lingered, and most Americans seemed willing to surrender their freedoms in order to be safe from terrorism. When an August 2003 Gallup poll, for example, asked whether the Bush administration had gone too far in restricting people's civil liberties to fight terrorism, the majority of respondents (55 percent) said that the administration's actions were about right, and only 21 percent responded that Bush had gone too far.

However, when asked if "the government [should] take all steps necessary to prevent additional acts of terrorism in the U.S. even if it means your basic civil liberties would be violated,"[30] 67 percent said that the government should take steps to prevent terrorism but should not violate civil liberties. This apparent inconsistency might be explained by yet another response in the survey: Half of those responding to the 2003 poll said they were not yet very familiar with the Patriot Act. As *Slate* editors Dahlia Lithwick and Julia Turner suggested in September 2003, the various lawsuits and criticisms of the Patriot Act at this point had only slowly begun to seep into the national consciousness, and Americans were just starting "to take a sober second look at what the act really unleashed."[31] As more information became available, the public became more knowledgeable about issues and more aware of the tradeoff between national security and constitutional freedoms.

Civil Liberties Versus National Security

The debate about the Patriot Act focused on the appropriate balance between protecting the civil liberties of Americans and enhancing national security. Attorney General John Ashcroft and other Bush administration officials described the changes made in the act as "modest and incremental"[32] and necessary to give the government the ability to protect national security and prevent another terrorist attack. Civil libertarians, on the other hand, claimed that the law threatened some of Americans' most important and fundamental freedoms. Four years after the act's passage, this debate was still continuing, partly because of the great secrecy built into many Patriot Act searches.

National Security Concerns

After the September 11, 2001, terrorist attacks, the U.S. government learned that the 9/11 terrorists had been living in the country for months while planning their attack, using library computers, cell phones, and other types of new technology to conduct research and communicate with each other. Some had even overstayed their visas, making them illegal immigrants who, if caught, could have been easily deported. Supporters said the Patriot Act was needed to modernize law enforcement and intelligence tools to enable government agencies such as the FBI and the CIA to detect potential terrorists in America and thereby prevent future terrorist attacks. As President Bush explained during the October 26 ceremony signing the bill into law:

> This law will give intelligence and law enforcement officials important new tools to fight a present danger. . . .

We're dealing with terrorists who operate by highly sophisticated methods and technologies, some of which were not even available when our existing laws were written. The bill before me takes account of the new realities and dangers posed by modern terrorists. It will help law enforcement to identify, to dismantle, to disrupt, and to punish terrorists before they strike.[33]

Sections 216's expanded power to search e-mails and Internet activity, for example, was a vital modernization, according to the president. He explained:

Surveillance of communications is . . . [an] essential tool to pursue and stop terrorists. The existing law was written in the era of rotary telephones. This new law . . . will

President George W. Bush speaks about the Patriot Act in 2005.

allow surveillance of all communications used by terrorists, including e-mails, the Internet, and cell phones. As
of today, we'll be able to better meet the technological
challenges posed by this proliferation of communications technology.[34]

The president also explained the rationale for Section 206's
roving wiretaps, stating: "Investigations are often slowed by limit
on the reach of federal search warrants. Law enforcement agencies have to get a new warrant for each new district they investigate, even when they're after the same suspect. Under this new
law, warrants are valid across all districts and across all states."[35]

NEITHER LIBERTY NOR SAFETY

"Those who would give up essential liberty to purchase a little
temporary safety deserve neither liberty nor safety."
—Benjamin Franklin, one of the founding fathers of the United
States and a leading American author, politician, printer,
scientist, philosopher, publisher, inventor, and diplomat
during the 1700s

Quoted in Constitutional Rights Foundation, "The Patriot Act: What Is the Proper
Balance Between National Security and Individual Rights?" www.crf-usa.org/terror/
patriot_act.htm.

Supporters also defended other parts of the Patriot Act as necessary to the nation's antiterrorism strategy. Section 215, for example,
was considered important for tracking terrorists' use of public computers. As former judge Kevin V. Ryan explained, "Congressional
testimony revealed that some of the Sept. 11 terrorists who hijacked
the plane that crashed into the Pentagon used computers in public
libraries weeks before the attack. We cannot allow libraries to become safe havens for criminals or terrorists to perform research or
communicate with each other or plan their attacks."[36] Supporters
said this provision would not be used to snoop on American citizens' reading habits, because the section expressly barred investigations of citizens for exercising their First Amendment rights.

A similar defense was advanced in support of the delayed notice provision in Section 213 for sneak-and-peek searches of

homes and properties. In order to delay notice, supporters pointed out, Section 213 required investigators to demonstrate to a judge that providing notice would have an adverse result such as endangering a person's life or safety, the destruction of evidence, the fleeing of a criminal suspect, the intimidation of witnesses, or the material compromise of an ongoing criminal investigation. Supporters said this requirement tempered Section 213 and made sneak-and-peek searches entirely reasonable given the country's need to fight terrorism.

According to the Justice Department, the Patriot Act simply allowed law enforcement agencies to use tools already available

The Bill of Rights

American civil liberties protections are found in the Bill of Rights, the first ten amendments to the U.S. Constitution, formally adopted on December 15, 1791. Some of the amendments central to the Patriot Act debate include:

- First Amendment—protects freedom of speech, association, religion, and the press.

- Fourth Amendment—protects Americans from unreasonable searches and seizures. It requires law-enforcement officers to obtain judicial warrants before making most searches, mandates that the government show probable cause that the targeted person has committed a crime, and requires warrants to be specific, "particularly

describing the place to be searched, and the persons or things to be searched."

- Fifth Amendment—guarantees due process of law, which usually means advance notice of a government action and an opportunity to challenge that action in a court or before some other competent authority.

- Sixth Amendment—requires a quick and fair trial in criminal matters.

- Eighth Amendment—requires that criminal defendants be released on bail unless they pose a danger to the community or present a risk that they will flee before trial.

for investigating organized crime and drug trafficking—a reference to the Racketeer Influenced and Corrupt Organizations Act, a law designed to facilitate criminal convictions of individuals involved with mafia organizations and drug rings. Bush administration officials promised that the government would use these new police powers against terrorists, not against American citizens. As Attorney General Ashcroft stated shortly after the law was enacted, "The American people can be assured law enforcement will use these new tools to protect our nation while upholding the sacred liberties expressed in the Constitution."[37]

A Threat to Democratic Freedoms

Despite the administration's assurances, civil rights advocates predicted that the Patriot Act's broad expansion of police powers would lead to infringement of civil liberties. Patriot Act opponents agreed that fighting terrorism was important and that existing surveillance laws needed updating in some areas, such as Internet and e-mail communications. They worried, however, that the act gave law enforcement and intelligence agents so much power that it would undermine basic American freedoms—such as the right to free speech and association guaranteed in the First Amendment, the right to privacy guaranteed by the Fourth Amendment, or the right to due process of law under the Fifth Amendment. As Senator Russell Feingold warned when Congress was considering the act:

> There is no doubt . . . that if we lived in a police state, it would be easier to catch terrorists. If we lived in a country where police were allowed to search your home at any time for any reason; . . . open your mail; eavesdrop on your phone conversations, or intercept your e-mail . . . the government would probably discover and arrest more terrorists. . . . But that would not be a country in which we would want to live.[38]

Critics basically saw the Patriot Act as an overreaction to the horrific events of 9/11. As law professor Geoffrey R. Stone argued: "War naturally generates a mood of fear and suspicion. Spies, saboteurs, and terrorists are seen lurking around every corner. . . . In

Opponents of the Patriot Act agree that surveillance laws for Internet and e-mail communications need updating.

light of the mood surrounding the passage of the PATRIOT Act only a month after 9/11, it was predictable that in at least some of its particulars the act would reach too far."[39] Even conservatives such as Phil Kent, president of the Southeastern Legal Foundation, expressed concerns that the act had overreached. He cautioned, "We must balance at all times the fact that national security is important, but freedom is essential."[40]

Instead of turning America into a police state, some critics argued, the war on terrorism should be fought largely by using law enforcement tools already available under U.S. criminal laws. A 2004 report by the 9/11 Commission—an independent, nonpartisan group set up to investigate the September 11, 2001, terrorist attacks—seemed to bolster this view. The commission found that the 9/11 attacks were caused primarily by intelligence failures, a lack of immigration enforcement, and lapses in airport security, and not by a lack of investigative powers such as those contained in the Patriot Act. Commissioners listed ten ways that authorities could have foiled the 9/11 attacks using existing law enforcement tools. The report also emphasized the need to protect civil liberties, stating:

> The burden of proof for retaining a particular governmental power should be on the executive, to explain (a) that the power actually materially enhances security and (b) that there is adequate supervision of the executive's use of the powers to ensure protection of civil liberties. If the power is granted, there must be adequate guidelines and oversight to properly confine its use.[41]

Ultimately, if the Patriot Act was permitted to erode American liberties, critics said, it would mean that the terrorists had won. As Senator Feingold said: "Preserving our freedom is one of the

The 9/11 Commission Report came out in 2004.

main reasons that we are now engaged in this new war on terrorism. We will lose that war without firing a shot if we sacrifice the liberties of the American people."[42]

Reduced Privacy

Many of the objections to the Patriot Act concerned threats to privacy guaranteed by the Fourth Amendment to the Constitution. This amendment prohibits unreasonable searches and seizures and requires police to obtain judicial warrants before conducting searches or surveillance. It authorizes judges to issue search warrants only if the government shows that there is probable cause that the targeted person has committed a crime. Under the Patriot Act, however, the FBI was granted enhanced powers to track e-mail and Internet usage, conduct sneak-and-peek searches of people's homes and businesses, obtain sensitive personal and financial records, and conduct nationwide roving wiretaps—all without probable cause. Critics also charged that the language of the act was not narrowly written to apply only to terrorists and that it allowed American citizens who had no connection to terrorism to be targeted. Once such broad powers were granted, critics said, law enforcement authorities could be expected to use them to the fullest extent possible. The Patriot Act, critics warned, could therefore open the door to a new era of domestic spying and privacy abuses by the federal government against ordinary American citizens.

Civil liberties advocates claimed, for example, that Section 213 sneak-and-peek searches reversed the principle of prior notice that has long been considered part of a reasonable search under the Fourth Amendment. If people are not given prior notice of a property search, advocates argued, they are not able to be present for the search, challenge deficiencies in the warrant, monitor whether the search is being conducted in accordance with the warrant, or obtain a receipt for items seized. Notably, too, Section 213 was not limited to terrorism investigations; it also was applied to criminal investigations. In addition, unlike some other parts of the act, this section was permanently authorized.

A number of other Title II sections, opponents said, expanded the reach of FISA searches in a manner that virtually gutted the

Fourth Amendment's search protections. Under the old FISA system, the FBI was limited to searches of business records in the possession of "a common carrier, public accommodation facility, physical storage facility, or vehicle rental facility,"[43] and only for the purpose of tracking down foreign spies. Critics said Section 215's new standards, which allowed searches for any tangible things as long as the search was part of an antiterrorism or intelligence investigation, were so loose that the government could search for all types of personal records and objects without ever showing that the target of the search was suspected of a crime, terrorist activity, or any other type of wrongdoing.

Furthermore, a FISA judge presented with a Section 215 application was required to enter an order as long as the application meets the requirements of the section, limiting judicial discretion. Also, while Section 215 barred investigations of persons solely because of First Amendment free speech activities, critics said this provision in reality provided very little protection be-

Shari Steele, the executive director of the civil liberties group Electronic Frontier Foundation, and one of her staff members are photographed at their office building.

cause agents could simply cite another reason for the search. Taken together, these provisions meant that authorities would almost always be granted an order to search for any items they wanted under Section 215. In fact, critics said the only way a FISA court would ever deny a records search under the language of Section 215 would be if the FBI bluntly stated that its search was based solely on First Amendment activities. The section's gag requirements, meanwhile, effectively prevented the targets of the searches from challenging them. Even worse was the fact that many Section 215–type records were searchable without even using Section 215 or obtaining FISA court permission—through FBI-issued NSLs, under Section 505.

FREEDOM VERSUS NATIONAL SECURITY

"It's important that the state be able to fight terror. No one disputes this. But it's equally important that the state not use the war on terror to gut the warrant requirement or undermine the First Amendment."

—Dahlia Lithwick and Julia Turner, senior editors at *Slate,*
an online political magazine

Dahlia Lithwick and Julia Turner, "A Guide to the Patriot Act," *Slate,* September 11, 2003. www.slate.com/id/2087984/.

Other Title II sections that enlarged the FBI's FISA electronic surveillance powers, critics said, allowed the government to monitor telephone and Internet communications throughout the United States, simply by asserting that the information was related to an intelligence or terrorism investigation. Access to e-mails and Web site data, for example, provided police with more content information than telephone records—everything from where people shop to what they read to who their friends are—without having to show probable cause under the Fourth Amendment. The authorization of roving wiretaps further enlarged police powers. Most significantly, critics said, the government could use this vastly expanded authority to spy on not just terrorists, but all residents. As the civil liberties group Electronic Frontier Foundation put it, "This gives the FBI a 'blank check' to violate the communications privacy of countless innocent Americans."[44]

Threats to Free Speech

Civil libertarians also were concerned about the act's effect on First Amendment rights to free speech and association. Critics attacked the definition of domestic terrorism in Section 802—"acts dangerous to human life that are a violation of the criminal laws" that "appear to be intended . . . to influence the policy of a government by intimidation or coercion"[45]—as extremely broad. They worried, for example, that acts of civil disobedience—deliberate violation of laws believed to be immoral or illegitimate—might be construed as illegal terrorist activities under the language of the act.

This would take away an important form of protest, they argued, and one that has been used throughout the nation's history by some of America's most notable activists. For example, Henry

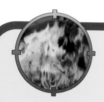

Past Civil Liberties Abuses

A number of commentators equated 9/11 and the Patriot Act with past instances where civil liberties were trampled during moments of crisis in American history. As early as 1798, a series of laws called the Alien and Sedition Acts were enacted in the name of defending the United States from its enemies. The laws made it illegal to "write, print, utter, or publish" anything critical of the president or Congress and allowed violators to be imprisoned for up to two years. Years later, a similar law—the Sedition Act of 1918—allowed some two thousand anti-war dissenters to be prosecuted during World War I. Passed at the urging of President Woodrow Wilson to prevent dissent about the war, this law made it illegal to use "disloyal, profane, scurrilous, or abusive language" about the U.S. government, flag, or armed forces during wartime. Finally, during World War II, under an executive order signed by President Franklin D. Roosevelt, 120,000 Americans of Japanese descent were forcibly imprisoned for fear they would help America's enemy, Japan. All of these actions were ultimately deemed, by the courts or other official acts, to be unconstitutional infringements of civil liberties.

David Thoreau refused to pay war taxes, Harriet Tubman ran an illegal Underground Railroad to free slaves, and Rosa Parks deliberately challenged racial segregation laws in the South. Certain groups that now use confrontational protest actions—such as environmental activists, antiglobalization activists, and antiabortion activists—were expected to be particularly vulnerable to prosecution or secret surveillance under the Patriot Act.

Opponents predicted that this definition of domestic terrorism would allow the government to target political activists and organizations based solely on their opposition to government policies—that is, based on the content of their political speech, which is protected by the First Amendment.

Threats to Immigrants

Critics warned, too, that the act would dramatically erode the rights of noncitizens. Section 411, for example, greatly expanded the class of immigrants who were subject to deportation on terrorism grounds. Although most people would define "terrorist activity" to mean politically motivated violence against civilians, Section 411 defined it as any crime that involves a weapon or other dangerous device—a definition that could allow the deportation of immigrants who have no connection to terrorism. Similarly, the section defined "engage in terrorist activity" and "terrorist organization" broadly, permitting immigrants to be deported even for contributing to lawful humanitarian activities—a result that critics argued violated immigrants' rights to freedom of association.

Section 412, meanwhile, gave the government the authority to jail suspects for as long as seven days based only on the government's certification that the person was engaged in terrorism or other activities that threaten the national security. If the person was charged with an immigration violation, he or she could then be held until the time of deportation. Persons who cannot be deported—for example, if no other country will accept them—could even be held indefinitely under the Patriot Act. The only type of judicial oversight was habeas corpus—a civil appeal available to prisoners for which the government is not required to provide free legal counsel. These low standards, critics said, fell far

Sami al-Hussayen was accused of providing material support for terrorism because of a link that he had on his Web site.

short of the Fourth Amendment's requirement of probable cause for an arrest or detention and violated the Fifth Amendment's requirement that no one should be deprived of their liberty without due process.

Civil Liberties Abuses

In the years after the Patriot Act's enactment, some of the worst fears of civil libertarians seemed to be coming true, as various media stories surfaced about government actions. Shortly after 9/11, the FBI began a nationwide effort to interview thousands of people that it said were potential witnesses, but many of those targeted were Muslims—a pattern critics said reflected an unfair and illegal government witch hunt. The government, for example, charged Idaho Muslim student and computer expert Sami al-Hussayen with providing material support for terrorism based solely on a link he used in building an Internet Web site. Al-Hussayen volunteered as a Web master for the Islamic Assembly of North America, and he posted Internet links on his Web site to terrorist fatwas, or declarations. Even though the Islamic Assembly was not designated as a terrorist group, and even though the same Internet links were posted on BBC news and other Web sites, the government charged that Al-Hussayen was giving expert advice to terrorists simply by posting the terrorist links. Critics said this violated Al-Hussayen's free speech rights. A jury later acquitted Al-Hussayen, accepting his First Amendment defense.

The government also used the Patriot Act to search secretly the Portland, Oregon, home of Muslim attorney Brandon Mayfield after the FBI wrongly concluded that his fingerprints matched those found at the scene of bombings in Madrid, Spain, in 2004. During the search, agents copied four computer hard drives, digitally photographed several documents, seized ten DNA samples, and took approximately 335 digital photographs. The secret search was possible only because of changes made by the Patriot Act. Mayfield was arrested as a material witness in the investigation of the Madrid incident but later was shown to be innocent of all charges.

Another Muslim, a widely respected European scholar named Tariq Ramadan, was prevented from accepting a professorship at Notre Dame when the government used Section 411 of the Patriot

Tariq Ramadan was denied admission to the United States by Section 411 of the Patriot Act.

Act to deny him admission to the United States. Ramadan is a moderate Islamic leader, and he had consistently condemned terrorism. However, he also had frequently criticized the Bush administration's policy in the Middle East, and many people believe he was barred solely due to his political views. Ramadan and others claimed this violated the First Amendment free speech protections.

Critics of the Patriot Act were alarmed, too, by the government's increasing use of secret NSLs. The heavily censored but lengthy NSL logs produced by the government in 2003, critics said, suggested that the FBI was relying on NSLs to avoid judicial oversight over the agency's surveillance efforts. The gag orders and delayed notice provisions in the Patriot Act prevented the recipients of NSLs and search warrants from revealing the searches, however, so detailed information about civil liberties abuses was kept secret from the public. Civil libertarians said this level of built-in secrecy in the act, combined with the government's stonewalling of congressional inquiries and Freedom of Information Act requests, made it impossible for Americans to know exactly how much their privacy had been compromised. As the ACLU explained, "An innocent American who may have had his or her home searched under a delayed notification 'sneak and peek' warrant, or had their medical records seized under Section 215 of the Patriot Act, would never know that these awesome powers have been misused against them."[46]

Patriot Act Successes

President Bush and Department of Justice officials, on the other hand, praised the Patriot Act for its successes in preventing terrorism. The administration claimed the Department of Justice had used the Patriot Act to charge more than 260 persons in terrorism investigations and that it secured guilty pleas or convictions in 140 of these cases. In addition, the government said it had disrupted terrorist cells around the country.

In Buffalo, New York, for example, six U.S. citizens of Yemeni descent pled guilty to providing material support to and receiving training from al Qaeda, the terrorist group responsible for the 9/11 terrorist attacks. In Seattle, Washington, Earnest James

Ujaama pleaded guilty to providing material support to the Taliban, the group in power in Afghanistan that was found to have given sanctuary to al Qaeda. In Portland, Oregon, people were charged with engaging in a conspiracy to join al Qaeda and Taliban forces fighting U.S. forces in Afghanistan. Similarly, in North Carolina, the government convicted members of a cell who provided material support to another Islamic terrorist group, Hizballah. In Tampa, Florida, eight individuals were indicted for their alleged support of yet another group—the Palestinian Islamic Jihad. Two individuals in Detroit were convicted of conspiring to support Islamic extremists plotting attacks in the United States, Jordan, and Turkey. In a September 2003 report, the White House concluded that the Patriot Act had helped the Justice Department thwart "potential terrorist activity throughout the United States."[47]

The trial of six suspected terrorists in Lackawanna, New York.

Administration officials argued that the civil liberties concerns of activists were unfounded. Attorney General Ashcroft frequently cited a July 31, 2003, Fox News poll showing that 91 percent of registered voters believed the Patriot Act had not affected their civil liberties. A 2004 Justice Department report concluded that the act had produced absolutely no civil rights abuses for American citizens. The report said that out of 1,266 civil rights and civil liberties complaints received by the department between June 15 and December 15, 2003, only 17 were found to merit a full investigation, and most of those involved allegations of excessive force, verbal abuse, and other alleged mistreatment of immigrants rather than citizens. Officials, meanwhile, defended the government's right to detain illegal immigrants who are suspected of involvement in terrorism. As Justice Department director of public affairs Barbara Comstock explained, "The simple fact is that illegal aliens who are not detained tend to flee."[48] Overall, Justice Department spokesman Mark Corallo argued, "It is clear that the government has been thoroughly responsible in its implementation of the [Patriot] act."[49] Years after its passage, no consensus about the Patriot Act had been reached.

A PERMANENT
PATRIOT ACT

Despite years of criticism, the Bush administration's support for the Patriot Act never wavered. As the four-year anniversary of 9/11 approached in 2005, the Bush administration lobbied hard for all of the Patriot Act's provisions to be made permanent; indeed, administration officials even tried to build support for stronger police powers. President Bush said: "This is no time to let our guard down, and no time to roll back good laws. . . . The Patriot Act is expected to expire, but the terrorist threats will not expire."[50] In the face of strong opposition, the administration ultimately convinced Congress to reauthorize the Patriot Act with only limited modifications.

Patriot Act II

The administration's effort to renew the Patriot Act began in January 2003, when the Justice Department leaked a copy of a revised version of the law called the Domestic Security Enhancement Act of 2003. The proposal, dubbed Patriot Act II by the press, contained more than one hundred new provisions that Justice Department spokesperson Mark Corallo said would "be filling in the holes of PATRIOT I . . . refining things that will enable us to do our job."[51] In August 2003, Attorney General Ashcroft launched a thirty-city, thirty-day U.S. tour to defend the original Patriot Act and try to sell the new proposal to the American public. He argued that if the Patriot Act had been in place earlier, 9/11 would not have happened and that the act helped to prevent more 9/11s during the two years it was in place. In a speech in August 2003, for example, Ashcroft said: "The cause we have chosen is just. The course we have chosen

In August 2003, Attorney General John Ashcroft toured the United States to promote a stronger Patriot Act.

is constitutional. The course we have chosen is preserving lives. . . . For two years, Americans have been safe. Because we are safer, our liberties are more secure."[52]

Critics attacked the administration's Patriot II proposal, however, claiming it would grant the federal government many new powers that would pose an even bigger threat to civil liberties. Among other things, civil rights advocates said the proposal would make it easier for the government to initiate surveillance and wiretaps on American citizens, allow the police to gather information on religious and political activities, and increase the availability of NSLs to search and seize information without a court warrant. Patriot II also, critics said, would make it harder to get information from the government through the Freedom of Information Act.

One provision in the proposal was singled out by critics as an example of Patriot II's excesses. Section 501, titled "Expatriation of Terrorists," would end the citizenship of American citizens who gave material support to the activities of organizations that the executive branch has deemed terrorist. Opponents said the definitions of "material support" and "terrorist organization" had already been broadened by Patriot I to include cases where people donate to humanitarian causes, and Patriot II's removal of citizenship for such activities was a frightening expansion of government power and an unconstitutional punishment for such activities.

A QUESTION OF TRUST

"The disclosure . . . that President Bush had authorized warrantless wiretapping of Americans for years [by the National Security Agency] showed once again that this is not an executive worthy of trust with open-ended powers."

—David Cole, law professor at Georgetown
University Law Center

David Cole, "Patriot Act Post-mortem, *Nation,* March 17, 2006. www.agenceglobal. com/article.asp?id=848.

The outcry against Patriot II caused it never to be formally introduced in Congress. In the fall of 2003, however, several bills were introduced containing provisions similar to the administration's proposal. Most of these bills failed to be enacted into law, but in December 2003, Congress passed an intelligence appropriations bill that quietly accomplished one of the changes President Bush sought in Patriot Act II—an expansion of NSL authority. Patriot Act I already allowed the FBI to use NSLs to obtain financial records from banks, credit unions, and other financial institutions without a court order. The new law, however, expanded the definition of "financial institution" to include twenty-six kinds of businesses, such as insurance companies, travel agencies, real estate agents, stockbrokers, the U.S. Postal Service, and even jewelry stores, casinos, and car dealerships. Before this change, the FBI had to acquire a court subpoena to obtain information from these sources, but the new law allowed the government to obtain information directly from businesses simply with an NSL request. President Bush signed the bill into law on December 13, 2003.

Samina Faheem, executive director of the American Muslim Voice, speaks out against the Patriot Act II.

The administration scored another victory in 2004 when Congress passed the Intelligence Reform and Terrorism Prevention Act (S 2845), also called the 9/11 Reform Act—legislation that implemented many of the recommendations of the 9/11 Commission for improving information sharing within the intelligence community and with state and local authorities. The legislation gained bipartisan support that ensured its passage, and the administration was able to insert language in the bill to expand FISA surveillance powers even beyond the limits of the original Patriot Act. This language, called the lone wolf provision, amended the definition of "agent of a foreign power" in FISA to allow intelligence investigations to use wiretaps and searches of suspected international terrorists not connected to a foreign government or organization. Critics said this was yet another weakening of the Fourth Amendment's search and seizure protections for noncitizens, but supporters claimed it was necessary to allow the government to pursue dangerous individuals who may not be connected to a particular country or terrorist organization.

The Reauthorization Debate

When Patriot Act II failed to gain legislative momentum, the Bush administration turned its attention to lobbying for congressional reauthorization of the provisions in Patriot I that were set to expire on December 31, 2005. These included some of the most controversial Patriot Act powers, such as roving wiretap authority, FISA pen/trap orders, and Section 215's any tangible thing provision, among others.

Reauthorization bills were introduced in both the House and the Senate, and in the period leading up to the 2005 deadline, Congress held extensive hearings on the issue and heard from more than sixty witnesses, including both administration supporters and civil liberties advocates. In the debates, defenders of the law largely repeated previous administration arguments that the Patriot Act had caused no significant constitutional or civil liberties abuses and that it merely updated surveillance and intelligence laws to fight terrorism. Republican House Judiciary Committee chairman F. James

Republican House Judiciary Committee chairman F. James Sensenbrenner defended the Patriot Act.

Sensenbrenner, for example, stated in floor debate that "there is no evidence that the Patriot Act has been used to violate civil liberties."[53] Texas Republican representative Louie Gohmert cited the terrorist arrest and conviction figures advanced by the Justice Department. New Mexico Republican Representative Heather Wilson even claimed—inaccurately—that the act was only used against foreigners and that the government still needs "a court order in order to get any business records or library records or anything else."[54]

The administration faced formidable opposition this time, however, not only from civil rights activists, but from a widespread movement composed of people from many different political perspectives. Members of Congress—both Democrats and Republicans—seemed much more willing to examine the Patriot Act than when it was first proposed. As reporter John Nichols said at the time, "Rarely in American history has a single law drawn such ideologically, politically and geographically diverse opposition."[55]

Patriot Act opponents contested administration claims that the act had been successful in combating terrorism and that no civil liberties abuses had been proven. Most of the successful terrorist convictions touted by the administration, critics said, consisted of guilty pleas to minor immigration violations or criminal offenses unrelated to terrorism. Many cases involved charges that defendants had provided material support to terrorist organizations—an allegation that critics said was so vague that it could mean almost anything. Some people reportedly were charged with this Patriot Act crime simply for attending a mosque where jihad (an Islamic word for holy war) was discussed or for giving money to Islamic charities that the government claimed were terrorist sympathizers. Even the prosecutions of so-called terrorist cells, critics said, involved very weak evidence against people with questionable links to terrorism.

One alleged terrorist cell in Lackawanna, New York, for example, involved six young men, all of them Muslim citizens. The men had grown up and gone to school in the United States, and they were all well-known and considered hardworking by their neighbors. In 2002, the FBI charged them with operating an al Qaeda terrorist cell and giving material support to terrorists. Following heavy surveillance authorized by the Patriot Act, the FBI's case rested on one fact—that the men had received weapons training in the spring of 2001 in Afghanistan, then the headquarters of al Qaeda, the terrorist group responsible for the 9/11 terrorist attack. In reality, however, the government never found any evidence that the men were terrorists or that they had any type of plan, plot, or intent to attack the United States or do any other type of harm.

All six men pleaded guilty to the charges and accepted sentences ranging from seven to ten years. Critics said, however,

A detainee is escorted into a processing tent at Guantánamo Bay. Critics of the alleged terrorist cell in Lackawanna, New York, say that the fear of being placed in a military prison might have led to their guilty plea.

that they were coerced into pleading guilty because the government implied that they otherwise would be charged as enemy combatants and placed in a military prison, where they might face indefinite detention or even the death penalty. Despite the lack of any evidence suggesting that this was truly a terrorist cell, administration officials hailed the Lackawanna case as a great victory in the war on terrorism. In his State of the Union address in January 2003, President Bush said, "We've broken al Qaeda cells in . . . Buffalo, New York. . . . We have the terrorists on the run."[56]

Legislative Defeat for Civil Liberties Advocates

Senator Russell Feingold, the lone Senate dissenter during the passage of Patriot Act I, became the leader of the reauthorization opposition in the Senate. He and his allies argued for a number of privacy protections, eventually convincing the Senate to approve unanimously a moderate reauthorization measure that helped to soften some of the most controversial provisions of the original Patriot Act. Some of the changes made by the Senate bill, called the USA PATRIOT Improvement and Reauthorization Act (S 1389), required the FBI to show that a person is involved with terrorism or spying before secretly obtaining library, medical, and other sensitive business records under Section 215. It also allowed recipients of Section 215 court orders to challenge them in court. In addition, the Senate legislation required the government to inform targets of sneak-and-peek searches within seven days, eliminated roving wiretaps,

The Case of Ahmed Omar Abu Ali

One alleged terrorist convicted by the government under the Patriot Act was Ahmed Omar Abu Ali, a young Arab-American raised in Falls Church, Virginia. Abu Ali was arrested by Saudi law enforcement authorities while taking final exams at a Saudi Arabian university in 2003. He was imprisoned by Saudi authorities for twenty months but never charged with a crime. Finally, in February 2005, Abu Ali was permitted to return to the United States, but only to face federal charges that he aided and abetted a conspiracy to commit terrorism. Charges were based on confessions Abu Ali made while in Saudi prison, to both Saudi and FBI investigators, but he challenged this evidence, claiming that he had not been permitted to talk to an attorney and had been tortured. A U.S. federal court permitted the confessions to be admitted into evidence, and a jury found Abu Ali guilty. On March 29, 2006, he was sentenced to thirty years in prison. Civil liberties critics called the case shocking and claimed that the U.S. government was holding suspects in foreign prisons in order to circumvent U.S. constitutional rights.

and once again made some of the most controversial parts of the Patriot Act temporary.

The House of Representatives, however, passed a version of the act favored by the administration and introduced by Representative F. James Sensenbrenner. Called the USA PATRIOT and Terrorism Prevention Reauthorization Act of 2005 (HR 3199), the House bill extended all of the provisions of the original Patriot Act and made them permanent simply by repealing the Section 224 sunset provision. Since the House and Senate bills were so different, a conference committee was charged with reconciling the two versions.

The final conference bill largely sided with the House version. It extended Section 215 only for four years and included some safeguards for the use of Section 215 and NSL searches, but Feingold and many others felt it still failed to address critical civil liberties flaws. As Senator Feingold reported: "The conference committee had the opportunity to fix many of the provisions of the Patriot Act to which Americans across the political spectrum have voiced their opposition over the last four years. . . . Unfortunately, they decided not to listen."[57] Feingold threatened to do everything he could to stop the Patriot Act reauthorization from becoming law.

A Temporary Extension

The House passed the conference bill, but before the Senate could vote on it, the legislative drive fell apart in December 2003 in the wake of news reports about other administration surveillance activities. Specifically, the news stories revealed that President Bush had signed an executive order in 2002 that authorized the National Security Agency (NSA), a supersecret U.S. intelligence agency, to spy on American citizens without first getting court search warrants. Administration officials confirmed that the president authorized the NSA to monitor Americans' phone calls and e-mail messages but said the authorization was limited to international calls and granted to track potential terrorists. Many experts, however, claimed the president's action violated the law, since the NSA is generally barred from any type of domestic spying unless it has court approval.

The NSA revelations added to the fears of Patriot Act critics, who already questioned the administration's commitment to ensuring privacy and civil liberties during its war on terrorism. Even Senator Arlen Specter, the Republican chair of the Senate Judiciary Committee, called the NSA spying "clearly and categorically wrong"[58] and promised to hold hearings on the matter. Ultimately, the NSA story helped Senator Feingold and his allies gain enough votes for a filibuster, a legislative tactic of continuous debate, that allowed them to block the Senate from voting on the conference committee's Patriot Act reauthorization bill. A Senate vote on December 17, 2005, fell seven votes short of the sixty votes needed to end the filibuster and move the bill forward.

With hopes of a full reauthorization stalled and the December 31 sunset deadline looming, the Senate agreed instead to extend the Patriot Act's sunset provisions to give Congress time

A view of the Threat Operations Center of the National Security Agency in Maryland.

to consider more carefully the Patriot Act renewal legislation. The bipartisan bill, S 2167, was introduced by Republican senator John Sununu and Democratic senator Patrick Leahy and passed on December 21, 2005, to extend the Patriot Act for six months. The House rejected the six-month extension and substituted a one-month extension, which the U.S. Senate quickly approved. The legislation ensured that the sunsetted provisions of the original Patriot Act would remain in effect until February 3, 2006. Congress later extended the date another five weeks to March 10, 2006.

The Patriot Act Renewed

The Patriot Act extension gave legislators time to discuss civil liberties objections and negotiate their differences with the Bush administration, but it did not ultimately stop the act's reauthorization. In February 2006, Bush officials and legislative leaders agreed to a compromise proposal that they believed would pass both the House and the Senate. The compromise became possible largely because a few key Republican senators such as John Sununu of New Hampshire, Larry E. Craig of Idaho, Lisa Murkowski of Alaska, and Chuck Hagel of Nebraska dropped their opposition to the bill after the administration agreed to several civil liberties modifications. The revised legislation garnered enough votes to defeat Senator Feingold's filibuster, and the reauthorization was quickly approved by both houses and signed into law by the president on March 9, 2006. The president praised the reauthorized Patriot Act, saying it was "vital to win the war on terror and to protect the American people."[59]

The reauthorization legislation repealed the original act's Section 224 sunset provision and made fourteen out of sixteen of the expiring provisions of the original Patriot Act permanent. Most of the Title II surveillance provisions were permanently renewed. Only two sections of the original law—Section 206, which provided for roving wiretaps, and Section 215, which authorized FISA searches for any tangible thing—were reauthorized on a temporary, four-year basis, with a new sunset date of December 31, 2009. The law extended the 2004 lone wolf amendment to FISA to the same 2009 date.

Civil Liberties Safeguards

Despite the failure of many of Senator Feingold's proposals, the reauthorized Patriot Act provided for a variety of civil liberty safeguards. The new law, for example, contained numerous restrictions on Section 215 searches. Law enforcement requests for Section 215 records now had to be personally approved by one of three top government officials—the FBI director, the deputy FBI director, or the executive assistant director for national security. Requests for Section 215 records also had to be explained by a statement of facts describing how the records were relevant to a terrorism or foreign intelligence investigation, and FISA judges were explicitly given the discretion to deny search requests. In addition, targets of 215 orders were now permitted to challenge the orders judicially, and the law explicitly stated that targets of 215 orders could talk to an attorney or others as necessary to challenge or comply with the order. Recipients were also allowed to ask a court to lift Section 215's gag provisions after one year.

CHANGES PROVIDE CLARITY

"Most of the changes made by . . . [the reauthorized Patriot Act] provide needed clarity to the original legislation. These modifications should convince critics that the Act is not a threat to our liberty but a means of protecting it."

—Wendy J. Keefer, former senior counsel and chief of staff in the U.S. Department of Justice Office of Legal Policy and now with Bancroft Associates in Washington, D.C.

Wendy J. Keefer, "The Patriot Act Reauthorized," *Jurist*, March 9, 2006. http://jurist. law.pitt.edu/forumy/2006/03/patriot-act-reauthorized.php.

Many of the other safeguards in the new Patriot Act concerned Section 505 and National Security Letters (NSLs). For example, the act provided that NSLs could now be challenged in court, and that recipients could discuss NSL orders with an attorney or others to comply with or challenge them. In addition, the NSL gag requirement only attached if the government certified that disclosure would cause a specific harm, and recipients could now

(Left to right) Senators John Sununu, Russ Feingold, and Lisa Murkowski discuss the Patriot Act. Several Republican senators such as Sununu and Murkowski dropped their opposition to the bill after a compromise was made.

challenge the gag order in federal court. Libraries operating in their traditional roles, as providers of books and basic Internet services, were specifically exempted from NSLs under the new law.

Still other safeguards clarified the rules for Section 213 sneak-and-peek property searches and roving wiretaps. The law now set a limit of thirty days for delayed notices of Section 213 searches and allowed courts to extend the delay for up to ninety days. To acquire the extension, however, the government had to present evidence showing the necessity for the delay. A number of restrictions were also placed on roving wiretaps, including: requirements for greater specificity in the government's application and in the orders themselves; for government investigators to inform the FISA court within ten days when the roving surveillance authority was used to target a new facility; and for the FISA court to be informed on an ongoing basis of the total number of places or facilities under surveillance. The authority for roving wiretaps was extended only for four years.

In addition, the new Patriot Act contained provisions for greater congressional and public oversight. The Justice Department was ordered to keep track of and publicly report on an annual basis the number of NSLs requested; the number of Section 215 applications submitted, approved, modified, and denied; as well as the number of applications for delayed notice

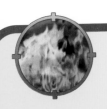

The NSA Wiretapping Scandal

In 2001, President Bush secretly authorized the National Security Agency (NSA) to monitor the international phone and e-mail communications of Americans without first obtaining a court warrant. The president defended the program as necessary to track down potential terrorists who may be making calls overseas, but critics said the action was a direct violation of the law, which generally prohibits the NSA from domestic spying. The NSA program was challenged in court by the American Civil Liberties Union and other civil rights organizations, and in August 2006, a Michigan federal court ruled that the warrantless NSA eavesdropping was a violation of the Fourth and First Amend-ments, FISA, and Title III. The court rejected the administration's claim that the president has inherent power to order wiretaps without a court order if national security is at stake, stating: "There are no hereditary Kings in America and no powers not created by the Constitution." The government planned to appeal the decision, but in January 2007 officials abruptly announced the NSA program would be terminated and replaced with one that obtains warrants through the FISA court.

ACLU v. National Security Agency, Memorandum Opinion, August 17, 2006. http://i.a.cnn\.net/cnn/2006/images/08/17/nsa.lawsuit.pdf.

sneak-and-peek searches. The act also required the Justice Department to provide Congress with classified information about its use of NSLs and its development of any large-scale data-mining programs—a term that refers to the process of digging through tons of information to discover patterns that might reveal evidence of terrorist or other unlawful activities.

President Bush, however, issued a statement called a signing statement at the time he signed the bill, indicating that he would not feel bound to comply with these reporting requirements. The statement asserted that the president could withhold information from Congress and the public if disclosure "could impair foreign relations, national security, the deliberative processes of the Executive, or the performance of the Executive's constitutional duties."[60] The statement, many commentators suggested, showed the administration intended to continue its pattern of concealing information about its use of surveillance powers under the act. Senator Patrick Leahy, for example, called the statement "nothing short of a radical effort to manipulate the constitutional separation of powers and evade accountability and responsibility for following the law." He added, "The president's constitutional duty is to faithfully execute the laws as written by the Congress, not cherry-pick the laws he decides he wants to follow."[61]

The Patriot Act was thus reauthorized with more civil rights restrictions than the original law, but administration critics and civil libertarians remained fearful that its broad police surveillance powers could still be used for purposes other than fighting terrorism, in ways that curtailed fundamental American freedoms. Opponents of the act vowed to continue their efforts to monitor the act's implementation for abuses and fight for constitutional liberties.

THE DEBATE CONTINUES

The reauthorization of the Patriot Act removed the issue from the forefront of congressional battles and daily news reports, but it did not settle the important, underlying disagreements about the appropriate balance between civil liberties and national security in an age of terrorism. The debate continues today as critics persist in their battle against the law and as public awareness about government surveillance grows.

Continuing Controversy

Bush administration officials and supporters praised the reauthorized Patriot Act, lauded its civil rights safeguards, and continued to claim that broad surveillance powers were necessary to help the government prevent terrorism. Former attorney general John Ashcroft, who resigned in 2004, defended the new Act as "narrowly tailored" and maintained it would "sustain the liberty and freedom of the people of the United States rather than threaten it."[62] Alberto R. Gonzales, the nation's new Attorney General, said the bipartisan reauthorization reflected a congressional consensus that the Patriot Act was necessary in the war on terror and demonstrated "that the Department of Justice had used the investigative tools provided by the Act in a responsible manner."[63] President Bush offered a now-familiar warning: "The terrorists have not lost the will or the ability to attack us. The Patriot Act is vital to the war on terror and defending our citizens against a ruthless enemy."[64]

Civil rights groups and other opponents, on the other hand, saw the act's reauthorization as a huge disappointment and vowed to press for more reforms. At the same time, many critics were glad that there was at least no further erosion of civil liberties. For example, Caroline Fredrickson, director of the ACLU Washington Legislative Office, said:

> The Patriot Act debate is far from over. . . . While Congress failed to adopt much-needed reforms to the law to better protect freedom and privacy, lawmakers also rejected pressure from the White House to include significant and unwarranted expansions of government power. We applaud those fair-minded lawmakers that have fought to bring the law in line with the Constitution, and together, we will continue to push for reforms to keep America safe and free."[65]

Attorney General Alberto Gonzales speaks about the renewal of the Patriot Act.

Major Flaws Remain

Critics argued that the civil rights safeguards in the renewed Patriot Act were largely cosmetic and that the act continued to embody major flaws. As the ACLU explained, the reauthorization bill "retains the most serious flaws from the original Patriot Act, primarily failing to require that any private records sought in an intelligence investigation be about suspected foreign terrorists or Americans conspiring with them."[66] The group noted, for example, that no significant changes were made to the sneak-and-peek search warrant power, and that this provision was being used not only against terrorism suspects but also in routine criminal investigations. In addition, although a number of restrictions were placed on Section 215 searches, the ACLU said the criteria for authorizing these searches—"to protect against international terrorism or clandestine intelligence activities"[67]—was still stacked in favor of the government. The group criticized, in particular, the Bush administration's rejection of proposals expressly to allow doctors, lawyers, and priests to challenge government efforts to acquire privileged communications from clients, patients, and church members.

DISTURBING ASSERTION

"[The] president's . . . assertion that he alone can safeguard our civil liberties isn't just disturbing and wrong. It's downright un-American."

—Jacob Weisberg, editor of *Slate*, an online political magazine, and coauthor, with Robert E. Rubin, of *In an Uncertain World*

Jacob Weisberg, "The Power-Madness of King George," *Slate*, January 25, 2006. www.slate.com/id/2134845/.

Indeed, the ACLU said even some of the so-called safeguards violated Americans' constitutional rights. The standard set forth for lifting gag orders accompanying NSLs and Section 215 searches, for example, allowed the government simply to assert that national security would be harmed if the gag order was lifted, and it required judges to accept this claim unless the person seeking to lift the gag order proved it was made in bad

A pedestrian looks at a sign in the window of a bookstore that states "Your First Amendment Needs You!" The ACLU maintains that the renewed Patriot Act still has flaws and certain areas violate First Amendment rights.

faith. This made it almost impossible to challenge gag orders, and the ACLU maintained this was a continuing violation of First Amendment rights.

Constitutional expert David Cole echoed these concerns. He noted that all sixteen provisions that were originally set to expire were extended, with only "minor modifications to a handful." He explained, "The Section 215 power remains incredibly broad; it doesn't even require the government to show that the person whose records are sought has any connection to terrorist activity." Cole argued, however, that

> the principal problem with the reauthorization debate was that most of the act's worst provisions were not even on the table. These include sections making it a crime to offer "expert advice" to a proscribed political group, regardless of its content; allowing the government to freeze the assets of suspected charities without any showing of wrongdoing, and based on secret evidence; and permitting foreign nationals to be locked up without charges, deported for innocent political associations and kept out of the country for endorsing any group the government labels as "terrorist"—under a definition so capacious that it could include the African National Congress and the Israeli military.[68]

Cole blamed the reauthorization failures on the Republican-dominated Congress, which he said was giving President Bush "a blank check on warrantless wiretapping instead of censuring him for . . . criminal spying."[69]

Continued Scrutiny of Civil Rights Abuses

Critics' concerns about the reauthorized Patriot Act only increased after its passage, when the government released information about some of its 2005 surveillance activities under the act. In an April 2006 report, the Department of Justice disclosed that the FBI in 2005 had issued more than 9,200 NSLs, seeking detailed information about more than 3,500 U.S. citizens and legal residents. The report was mandated by new provisions enacted in the reauthorization bill and marked the first time the

The FBI collected information on several antiwar groups, including the peace group Raging Grannies.

government provided an official count of its NSL activities; previously, the Department of Justice had refused to provide information to Congress on NSLs. The Justice Department report also revealed a total of 2,072 secret search warrants under FISA in 2005—a striking 18 percent increase from the year before. Critics said these new statistics showed that the government had been rapidly expanding its surveillance activities under the Patriot Act. As Caroline Fredrickson of the ACLU stated: "This tells us why they didn't want to tell us in the past how many of these they were actually using. . . . The idea that this kind of power resides in the hands of so many people at the FBI with no court oversight is very troubling."[70]

Additional concerns developed when information came to light that indicated the FBI was using the Patriot Act to conduct investigations of political organizations based solely on their antiwar political views—surveillance activities that critics said constituted clear violations of free speech and association. According to documents obtained by the ACLU through the Freedom of Information

FBI director Robert Mueller testifies before the Senate Judiciary Committee on May 2, 2006.

Act, for example, the FBI initiated a classified investigation into the activities of the Thomas Merton Center, an organization that conducts nonviolent protests and advocates on behalf of peace and justice issues. A November 2002 FBI memo contained in the Freedom of Information Act documents referred to an "investigation on Pittsburgh anti-war activities," described the center as "a left-wing organization advocating, among many political causes, pacifism," and reported that it "holds daily leaflet distribution activities in downtown Pittsburgh and is currently focused on its opposition to the potential war on Iraq."[71]

Later Freedom of Information Act disclosures revealed that the FBI was collecting information on a number of other peaceful antiwar groups as well, including various Quaker and student groups. The FBI even investigated the Raging Grannies, an organization of aging activists who use peaceful sit-ins, songs,

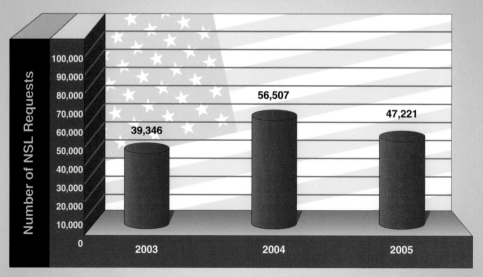

Number of NSL (National Security Letter) Requests, 2003–2005

NSLs are secret FBI warrants originally designed to get limited types of electronic telephone and banking records. The Patriot Act significantly expanded the types of records the FBI could obtain with these warrants.

Number of NSL Requests

- 100,000
- 90,000
- 80,000
- 70,000
- 60,000
- 50,000
- 40,000
- 30,000
- 20,000
- 10,000
- 0

2003: 39,346
2004: 56,507
2005: 47,221

Source: U.S. Department of Justice, *A Review of the Federal Bureau of Investigation's Use of National Security Letters*, March 2007. Available online at http://www.npr.org/documents/2007/mar/doj/doj_oig_nsl.pdf.

and satire to protest the Iraq war. Ann Beeson, associate legal director of the national ACLU, warned: "This administration has embarked on an unprecedented campaign to spy on innocent Americans. . . . Investigating law-abiding groups and their members simply because of their political views . . . has a chilling effect on the vibrant tradition of dissent in this country."[72]

PATRIOT ACT DOES NOT WORK

"The Patriot Act has come to symbolize an overstepping of the executive branch's power. Unfortunately, that image is based largely on misinformation."
—Paul Rosenzweig, Alane Kochems, and James Jay Carafano, researchers at The Heritage Foundation, a conservative think tank

Paul Rosenzweig, Alane Kochems, and James Jay Carafano, "The Patriot Act Reader: Understanding the Law's Role in the Global War on Terrorism," Heritage Foundation, September 13, 2004. www.heritage.org/Research/HomelandDefense/The-Patriot-Act-Reader.cfm.

In the wake of some of these disclosures, the Senate Judiciary Committee held oversight hearings on the Patriot Act in May of 2006. Senators grilled FBI director Robert Mueller about the FBI's use of the surveillance powers under the act, including the agency's monitoring of antiwar groups. In the case of the Thomas Merton Center, Mueller explained that the FBI was really targeting one particular suspect in the group, rather than the group's antiwar activities. Senator Patrick Leahy, then the ranking Democrat on the committee, however, noted that the FBI's own memo specifically described the purpose of the investigation as tracking antiwar activities. Leahy said, "I'm very disappointed when I find that the FBI has been using new [Patriot Act] capabilities against Americans simply because they oppose the war in Iraq."[73] Senators also questioned the NSL numbers, expressing concerns that so much surveillance activity was taking place without any judicial review. As Senator Russell Feingold commented, after noting that the number of NSL requests was far larger than the 155 requests made under Section 215, "I fear the reason might be that in Section 215 they have to go before a judge, and with national security letters, they don't."[74]

Developments in Legal Challenges

Civil libertarians also continued their efforts to challenge the Patriot Act in the courts. As the ACLU explained, "Reauthorization does not make the Patriot Act constitutional."[75] Following reauthorization, for example, the ACLU continued to press its arguments in *Doe and ACLU v. Ashcroft et al.*, a lawsuit that it began in 2004 challenging the constitutionality of the Patriot Act's NSL provision, Section 505. A federal district court ruled in the ACLU's favor in September 2004, but the government appealed the case. Before the federal appellate court could rule, however, the Patriot Act was reauthorized and the appeals court sent the case back to the district court, asking it to rule on the constitutionality of the reauthorized act. Appellate judge Richard Cardamone, however, strongly criticized the government's arguments in a separate concurring opinion, saying: "A ban on speech and a shroud of secrecy in perpetuity are antithetical to democratic concepts and do not fit comfortably with the fundamental rights guaranteed American citizens. . . . Unending secrecy of actions taken by government officials may also serve as a cover for possible official misconduct and/or incompetence." National security concerns, Cardamone added, "should be leavened with common sense so as not forever to trump the rights of the citizenry under the Constitution."[76]

The ACLU's client in this case, an anonymous Internet provider, remained secret under Section 505's gag provision. Although Congress fixed some of the problems with Section 505, the ACLU argues that the gag provision is an unconstitutional violation of the First Amendment because the statute still requires courts to defer to the FBI's judgment about when a gag order is necessary. As Jameel Jaffer, the lead ACLU lawyer in the case, explained: "The secrecy surrounding the FBI's use of national security letters is excessive and dangerous. . . . By permitting the FBI to operate without meaningful public or judicial oversight, Congress has undermined important safeguards against abuse."[77]

In a second ACLU case challenging NSLs, *ACLU v. Gonzales et al.*, however, the government released its gag order and then

Gagged Librarians Speak Out

After the government lifted its gag order on four librarians who challenged the constitutionality of National Security Letters in *ACLU v. Gonzales et al.*, the librarians spoke out for the first time about their ordeal. Peter Chase, vice president of a library consortium in Connecticut, explained his reasons for suing the government in a May 30, 2006, statement published on the American Civil Liberties Union Web site:

> As a librarian, I believe it is my duty and responsibility to speak out about any infringement to the intellectual freedom of library patrons. . . . The government was telling Congress that it didn't use the Patriot Act against libraries and that no one's rights had been violated. I felt that I just could not be part of this fraud being foisted on our nation. We had to defend our patrons and ourselves, and so, represented by the ACLU [American Civil Liberties Union], we filed a lawsuit challenging the government's power to demand these records without a court order. . . . The battle continues, but at least now we can speak out publicly about our fight to preserve the freedoms that we all hold dear.

Quoted in American Civil Liberties Union, *"Doe v. Gonzales:* Fighting the FBI's Demand for Library Records—Statement of Peter Chase," May 30, 2006. www.aclu.org/safefree/nationalsecurityletters/25698res20060530.html.

Peter Chase, vice president of Library Connection, Inc., a library consortium in Connecticut, speaks about the consortium's battle against Patriot Act demands. They sought help from the ACLU.

withdrew its NSL request completely following several months of litigation. The case involved four librarians on the board of Library Connection, a library consortium in Connecticut that was served with an NSL. The ACLU challenged both the letter and the accompanying gag order. ACLU spokesperson Ann Beeson claimed victory in the case, stating:

> First the government abandoned the gag order that would have silenced four librarians for the rest of their lives, and now they've abandoned their demand for library records entirely. . . . While the government's real motives in this case have been questionable from the beginning, their decision to back down is a victory not just for librarians but for all Americans who value their privacy.[78]

The ACLU also joined several other groups in challenging the government's refusal to issue a visa to Muslim scholar Tariq Ramadan under Section 411 of the Patriot Act. Section 411 allows the government to refuse admission to persons who "endorse or espouse terrorist activity,"[79] but Ramadan and his supporters argued that the visa refusal was instead based on his political views, which have been critical of the Bush administration. The lawsuit alleged that the government's exclusion of Ramadan simply because of his political views was a violation of the First Amendment's free speech guarantees. In a June 2006 decision, a federal district court in New York agreed with the ACLU's position, ruling that the government cannot exclude people from the United States solely because it "disagrees with the content of the alien's speech and therefore wants to prevent the alien from sharing this speech with a willing American audience."[80] Judge Paul Crotty explained, "The First Amendment rights of American citizens are implicated when the Government excludes an alien from the United States on the basis of his political views."[81]

A Campaign for Strong Executive Power

As time passed, many Patriot Act critics began to see the Patriot Act as part of a much larger campaign by the Bush administration to expand the power of the presidency and the executive branch of government. The revelations of NSA surveillance, in particular, caused many people to fear that President Bush sought to make himself the final arbiter of what the law is, without regard to the restrictions of the Constitution, Congress, or the courts. Although many legal analysts said domestic spying is illegal except as authorized in FISA, the administration justified giving the order for secret domestic NSA spying by arguing that it was implicit in Congress's limited authorization of military force after 9/11 and part of the president's inherent war powers. The president thus seemed to be claiming unlimited war powers to fight terrorism, even if that meant ignoring U.S. laws. Commentator Bruce Schneier warned, "This is indefinite dictatorial power . . . the very definition of a dictatorship is a system that puts a ruler above the law."[82]

Journalist Elizabeth Drew explained that Bush's idea of broad presidential power is derived from a concept of the "unitary executive,"[83] which holds that a president may overrule the courts and Congress based on presidential interpretations of the Constitution. Bush has used this concept of expanded presidential powers on many different occasions. In fact, according

President George W. Bush has been accused of acting above the law after revelations of NSA surveillance.

to the *Boston Globe*, President Bush issued more than 750 signing statements during his presidency, claiming the right to ignore various laws passed by Congress. Traditionally, a president who does not agree with a law passed by Congress has the power to veto the legislation, but Congress could override the veto with enough votes. President Bush has never vetoed a bill; instead, he issues signing statements and uses them to ignore parts of laws he does not like. Reporter Charlie Savage says these signing statements have been used to avoid "military rules and regulations, affirmative-action provisions, requirements that Congress be told about immigration services problems, 'whistle-blower' protections for nuclear regulatory officials, and safeguards against political interference in federally funded research."[84]

"A SURVEILLANCE SOCIETY"

"Privacy and liberty in the United States are at risk. A combination of lightning-fast technological innovation and the erosion of privacy protections threatens to transform Big Brother . . . into a very real part of American life."

—Jay Stanley and Barry Steinhardt, policy analysts at the
American Civil Liberties Union

Quoted in M. Katherine B. Darmer, Robert M. Baird, and Stuart E. Rosenbaum, eds., *Civil Liberties vs. National Security in a Post-9/11 World.* Amherst, NY: Prometheus, 2004, p. 54.

The push for broad executive power, however, was most pronounced in the war on terror. In addition to authorizing domestic NSA surveillance and reserving the right to interpret parts of the Patriot Act, the administration detained nearly five hundred terrorist suspects, called enemy combatants, in Guantánamo Bay, Cuba, without charging them of a crime—a decision that many experts warned was a violation of both the U.S. Constitution and the Geneva Conventions, international treaties that govern the treatment of prisoners of war. Another well-known example of expanding presidential power was a signing statement that Bush added to a law sponsored by Republican senator John McCain and passed by both houses of Congress

Hundreds of terrorist suspects are detained in Guantánamo Bay, Cuba.

banning cruel, inhuman, or degrading treatment of terrorist detainees. Critics said Bush, in effect, claimed to reserve the right to order torture despite the statute's explicit ban.

Opponents said these actions by the president made the battle for civil liberties reforms in the Patriot Act almost irrelevant, since the administration seemed to be claiming the right to conduct surveillance on Americans or take any other action in the war on terror regardless of what is permitted under law and regardless of how it affects fundamental constitutional values. As the ACLU explained, "Even if we were to win all of the reforms needed to fix the Patriot Act, until Americans demand that the president be required to follow the law, any such changes could be ignored under the current regime."[85]

The Future of the Patriot Act

In the final years of the Bush presidency, the issue of the appropriate balance between civil liberties and national security remains undecided. Administration supporters continued to claim the president needs broad powers to fight the war on terror. Bush supporters defended the president's use of NSA surveillance, for example, as vital for national security because the president decided it was necessary to monitor international calls to spot potential terrorist threats. As William Kristol, editor of the *Weekly Standard*, said, "A unitary chief executive . . . [can], in times of war or emergency, act with the decisiveness, dispatch and, yes, secrecy, needed to protect the country and its citizens."[86]

Other Americans, however, thought that antiterrorism measures were unreasonably curtailing constitutional liberties. Although the Patriot Act may have been enacted based on well-meaning motives of combating the evils of terrorism, the war

The issue of balancing civil liberties and national security remains undecided. In 2006, Secretary of Defense Donald Rumsfeld admitted that the war on terror could last for years.

on terror seemed to have no end. As Louis Fisher, a separation-of-powers expert at the Congressional Research Service, explained: "It is one thing to hold your breath for a couple of years and hope the administration isn't going to abuse its power . . . but this [the war on terror] is probably going to go a lot longer than any war we've ever had."[87] In 2006, in fact, Secretary of Defense Donald Rumsfeld admitted the war on terror could last for decades. This raised concerns that the changes wrought by the Patriot Act and Bush's claim of broad executive power might create permanent limitations on constitutional freedoms. Some commentators even suggested that the matter had risen to the level of a constitutional crisis. As Elizabeth Drew warned in 2006, "For the first time in more than thirty years [since the Watergate scandal], and to a greater extent than even then, our constitutional form of government is in jeopardy."[88]

Patriot Act Is a Success

"The success of our intelligence and law enforcement officials in preventing another terrorist attack on the American homeland would not have been possible without the tools that Congress gave them in the USA Patriot Act."

—Viet D. Dinh, former assistant U.S. attorney at the Department of Justice

Quoted in Terry Rombeck, "Patriot Act Author Defends Law as Terror-Fighting Tool," LJWorld.com, September 11, 2004. www2.ljworld.com/news/2004/sep/11/patriot_act_author/.

The future of the Patriot Act and other presidential bids for power may depend on the responses of other branches of government, and ultimately on the public's view of the government's actions. Based on the record so far, the best possibility of further reforms of Patriot Act surveillance powers may lie with the courts, since several federal courts have ruled parts of the act unconstitutional. The Supreme Court also checked the president's bid for broad executive powers in two recent cases. In *Rasul v. Bush* (2004), the Court ruled that American courts had the authority to decide whether foreign terror suspects held at Guantánamo Bay had been rightfully detained, and in *Hamdan v. Rumsfeld* (2006), the Court held that military commissions set up by the administration to try detainees held at Guantánamo Bay violated the Geneva Conventions and lacked constitutional due process protections.

Prior to the 2006 congressional elections, however, most members of the Republican-controlled Congress showed little interest in challenging the administration on matters relating to the war on terror. Following the *Hamdan* ruling, Congress even passed a bill giving Bush the authority he requested to detain terrorist suspects indefinitely, try them in military commissions, and prevent them from appealing to American courts. Legal experts, such as Yale law professor Bruce Ackerman, said the bill weakens the judiciary, "further entrenches presidential power,"[89] and potentially allows American citizens charged as terrorists to be separated from their constitutional rights. Commentators

George Orwell's *1984*

Many commentators on the Patriot Act claim that it brings U.S. society closer to the model of a high-surveillance, totalitarian society portrayed by author George Orwell in his science fiction book, *1984*, published in 1949. In the book, Orwell describes a dark, futuristic world in which an authoritarian government, called Big Brother, is all-powerful and uses indoctrination, propaganda, and surveillance to control its citizens' every move. Orwell wrote the book as a satire to warn against the evils of dictatorial government, but critics of the Patriot Act point out several similarities between the book and modern-day America. For example, as in *1984*, the U.S. government is fighting an indefinite war against an amorphous enemy—the war on terror. Also, President Bush has fought to increase his own powers, which many argue is moving the country closer to a dictatorship. Meanwhile, under the Patriot Act, the government has acquired broad new powers to monitor phone conversations, Internet communications, business transactions, financial records, and a long list of other personal information. At the same time, critics say, the Patriot Act has eroded some of the most important constitutional safeguards against government search power, such as the Fourth Amendment's requirement of probable cause.

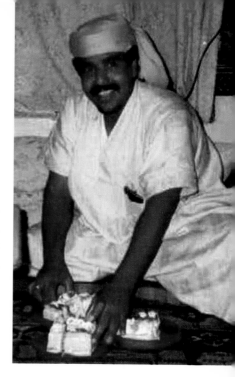

Salim Ahmed Hamdan is seen in this undated photo. He was the first detainee to appear before a U.S. Military Commission that prevents appeals.

suggested, however, that congressional willingness to go along with expanded presidential powers might diminish because Democrats won control of the House and Senate in the November 2006 elections. This theory gained support in January 2007, when the Bush administration abruptly disbanded the controversial NSA spy program and replaced it with one that would be subject to the FISA court.

In the end, the key may be the public's views about the degree of permissible governmental intrusion in the lives of Americans. Although large majorities of Americans favored liberal government surveillance powers immediately following the 9/11 terrorist attacks, a 2006 Zogby poll suggested that public attitudes may be changing. The new poll found that Americans are now "largely unwilling to surrender civil liberties—even if it is to prevent terrorists from carrying out attacks." The poll also found that "even routine security measures, like random searches of bags, purses, and other packages, were opposed by half (50 percent) of respondents in the survey . . . [and] just 28 percent are willing to allow their telephone conversations to be monitored."[90] Civil libertarians said this shift in public attitudes may signal that Americans are awakening to the dangers posed by new government surveillance powers. If the public does not object, however, critics say the United States may be entering a world of heightened surveillance. In such a world, Harvard Law School professor Laurence Tribe has warned, the government would be "behind every wall, behind every e-mail, and invisibly present in every electronic communication, telephonic or otherwise."[91]

Introduction: A Delicate Balance

1. Quoted in White House, "President Signs Anti-Terrorism Bill: Remarks at the Signing of the Patriot Act," October 26, 2001. www.whitehouse.gov/news/releases/2001/10/20011026-5.html.

Chapter 1: A Response to Terror

2. Quoted in Patriot Resource, "Weekly Radio Address," September 15, 2001. www.patriotresource.com/wtc/president/ 010915a.html.
3. Quoted in White House, "Address to a Joint Session of Congress and the American People," September 20, 2001. www. white house.gov/news/releases/2001/09/20010920-8.html.
4. Quoted in Robert O'Harrow Jr., "Six Weeks in Autumn," *Washington Post*, October 27, 2002. www.washingtonpost.com/ac2/wp-dyn?pagename=article&contentId=A19992002Oct22&notFound =true.
5. Quoted in Herbert N. Foerstel, *Refuge of a Scoundrel: The Patriot Act in Libraries*. Westport, CT: Libraries Unlimited, 2004, p. 54.
6. Quoted in Constitutional Rights Foundation, "America Responds to Terrorism: The Patriot Act: What Is the Proper Balance Between National Security and Individual Rights?" www.crf-usa.org/ter ror/patriot_act.htm.
7. *The Uniting and Strengthening America by Providing Appropriate Tools Required to Intercept and Obstruct Terrorism (USA PATRIOT ACT) Act of 2001*, HR 3162, 107th Congress, 1st session. www.epic. org/privacy/terrorism/hr3162.html.
8. O'Harrow, "Six Weeks in Autumn."
9. Foerstel, *Refuge of a Scoundrel*, p. 45.
10. James X. Dempsey and David Cole, *Terrorism & the Constitution: Sacrificing Civil Liberties in the Name of National Security*. New York: New Press, 2002, p. 107.
11. *The Uniting and Strengthening America by Providing Appropriate Tools Required to Intercept and Obstruct Terrorism (USA PATRIOT ACT) Act of 2001*.
12. *The Uniting and Strengthening America by Providing Appropriate Tools Required to Intercept and Obstruct Terrorism (USA PATRIOT ACT) Act of 2001*.

13. *The Uniting and Strengthening America by Providing Appropriate Tools Required to Intercept and Obstruct Terrorism (USA PATRIOT ACT) Act of 2001.*

Chapter 2: A Controversial Law

14. Quoted in Leigh S. Estabrook, "Public Libraries and Civil Liberties: A Profession Divided," Library Research Center, 2002. http://transcoder.usablenet.com/tt/lrc.lis.uiuc.edu/web/PLCL.html.
15. The American Library Association, "Resolution on the USA Patriot Act and Related Measures That Infringe on the Right of Library Users," 2002–2003 CD #20.1, 2003 ALA Midwinter Meeting. www.ala.org/ala/washoff/WOissues/civilliber ties/theusapatriot act/alaresolution.htm.
16. Foerstel, *Refuge of a Scoundrel*, p. 60.
17. Foerstel, *Refuge of a Scoundrel*, p. 61.
18. Quoted in Evelyn Nieves, "Local Officials Rise Up to Defy the Patriot Act," *Washington Post*, April 21, 2003. www.washingtonpost.com/ac2/wp-dyn?pagename=article&node=&contentId=A64173-2003Apr20&notFound=true.
19. Quoted in Bill of Rights Defense Committee Press Release, "BORDC Calls on Congress to Fix PATRIOT Act," March 2, 2006. www.bordc.org/press/pr-03-02-06.php.
20. Quoted in Kelley Beaucar Vlahos, "Local Communities Refuse to Enforce Patriot Act," Fox News.com, May 15, 2003. www.fox news.com/story/0,2933,86915,00.html.
21. Quoted in American Civil Liberties Union, "In ACLU Case, Federal Court Strikes Down Patriot Act Surveillance Power as Unconstitutional," September 29, 2004. www.aclu.org/safefree/spy ing/18589prs20040929.html.
22. Quoted in Humanitarian Law Project, "Key Patriot Act Provision Ruled Unconstitutional," 2004. http://hlp.home.igc.org/.
23. Quoted in Humanitarian Law Project, "Key Patriot Act Provision Ruled Unconstitutional."
24. Quoted in Humanitarian Law Project, "Key Patriot Act Provision Ruled Unconstitutional."
25. Quoted in American Civil Liberties Union, "In New Advertisement, ACLU Calls for Stop to Attorney General's Assault on Civil Liberties," February 6, 2003. www.aclu.org/safefree/general/171 56prs20030206.html.
26. Foerstel, *Refuge of a Scoundrel*, p. 138.
27. Quoted in Foerstel, *Refuge of a Scoundrel*, p. 138.
28. Quoted in Foerstel, *Refuge of a Scoundrel*, p. 146.
29. Quoted in Leah Sandwell-Weiss, "A Look at the Patriot Act Today," National Conference on Privacy and Public Access to Court

Records, July 2004. http://72.14.253.104/search? q=cache:ma9
prk1WwqIJ:www.aallnet.org/products/pub_sp0407/pub_sp0407_
PATRIOT.pdf+Humanitarian+Law+Project+v.+John+Ashcroft&hl=
en&gl=us&ct=clnk&cd=21.

30. Quoted in Constitutional Rights Foundation, "America Responds
to Terrorism."

31. Dahlia Lithwick and Julia Turner, "A Guide to the Patriot Act:
Should You Be Scared of the Patriot Act?" *Slate*, September 8, 2003.
www.slate.com/id/2087984/.

Chapter 3: Civil Liberties Versus National Security

32. Quoted in American Civil Liberties Union, "ACLU Says Justice
Dept.'s PATRIOT Act Website Creates New Myths About Controversial Law," August, 26, 2003. www.aclu.org/safe free/patriot/
16760prs20030826.html.

33. Quoted in White House, "Remarks at the White House Signing of
the USA Patriot Act of 2001," October 26, 2001. www.white
house.gov/news/releases/2001/10/20011026-5.html.

34. Quoted in White House, "Remarks at the White House Signing of
the USA Patriot Act of 2001."

35. Quoted in White House, "Remarks at the White House Signing of
the USA Patriot Act of 2001."

36. Kevin V. Ryan, "Why All Provisions of the Patriot Act Should Be
Reauthorized," *San Fransisco Chronicle*, May 9, 2005. www.sfgate.
com/cgibin/article.cgi?file=/chronicle/archive/2005/05/09/EDGM7
C904A1.DTL.

37. Quoted in PBS, "The Patriot Act: Is the Government Protecting
U.S. Citizens from Future Terrorist Attacks or Invading Their Privacy?" February 12, 2003. www.pbs.org/news hour/extra/fea
tures/jan-june03/patriot.html.

38. Russell Feingold, "Statement of U.S. Senator Russ Feingold on the
Anti-Terrorism Bill from the Senate Floor," Russ Feingold: United
States Senator, October 25, 2001. http://feingold.senate.gov/
speeches/01/10/102501at.html.

39. Quoted in *Legal Affairs*, "What's Wrong with the Patriot Act?" October 3, 2005. www.legalaffairs.org/webexclusive/debateclub_pat
act1005.msp.

40. Quoted in Vlahos, "Local Communities Refuse to Enforce Patriot
Act."

41. National Commission on Terrorist Attacks, "The 9/11 Commission
Report," July 22, 2004. www.9-11commission.gov/report/index.htm.

42. Quoted in Brigid O'Neil, "The PATRIOT Act's Assault on the Bill of
Rights," Independent Institute, September 15, 2003. www.inde
pendent.org/newsroom/article.asp?id=1184.

43. Effective Antiterrorism Tools for Law Enforcement Act of 1997, 18 U.S.C. § 2720(a).

44. Electronic Frontier Foundation, "Let the Sun Set on Patriot Section 206: 'Roving Surveillance Authority Under the Foreign Intelligence Surveillance Act of 1978.'" www.eff.org/patriot/sunset/206.php.

45. *The Uniting and Strengthening America by Providing Appropriate Tools Required to Intercept and Obstruct Terrorism (USA PATRIOT ACT) Act of 2001.*

46. American Civil Liberties Union, "Justice Department Issues Review of Civil Liberties Abuses, ACLU Says Patriot Act Still Remains Shrouded in Secrecy," March 8, 2006. www.aclu.org/safefree/general/24433prs20060308.html.

47. White House, "Progress Report on War on Terrorism: Attacking Terrorist Networks at Home and Abroad," September 2003. www.whitehouse.gov/homeland/progress/attacking.html.

48. Barbara Comstock, "Rhetoric vs. Reality," *National Review Online*, September 3, 2003. www.nationalreview.com/comment/comment-comstock090303.asp.

49. Quoted in NewsMax.com, "Department of Justice Finds No Abuses of Patriot Act," January 27, 2004. www.newsmax.com/archives/articles/2004/1/27/182823.shtml.

Chapter 4: A Permanent Patriot Act

50. Quoted in Brad Knickerbocker, "America Wrestles with Privacy vs. Security," *Christian Science Monitor*, July 22, 2005. www.csmonitor.com/2005/0722/p03s01uspo.html?s=widep.

51. Quoted in Matt Welch, "Get Ready for PATRIOT II," *AlterNet*, April 2, 2003. www.alternet.org/story/15541.

52. Quoted in Jeff Johnson, "Liberties Groups Slam Ashcroft's PATRIOT Act 'Roadshow,'" CNSNews.com, August 21, 2003. www.cnsnews.com/ViewPolitics.asp?Page=%5CPolitics%5Carchive%5C200308%5CPOL20030821a.html.

53. Quoted in Chip Pitts, "A Constitutional Disaster," *Nation*, November 7, 2005. www.thenation.com/doc/20051107/ pitts.

54. Quoted in Pitts, "A Constitutional Disaster."

55. John Nichols, "Blog: The Online Beat: Feingold to Fight Patriot Act Reauthorization," *Nation*, December 10, 2005. www.thenation.com/blogs/thebeat?pid=42017.

56. Quoted in White House, "State of the Union," January 28, 2003. www.whitehouse.gov/news/releases/2003/01/20030 128-19.html.

57. Quoted in Nichols, "Blog."

58. Quoted in Anne Marie Squeo and Neil King Jr., "Senate Blocks Patriot Act Renewals: Vote Deals Setback to Bush as Antiterrorist Law

Spurs Privacy Concerns," *Wall Street Journal*, December 17, 2005. http://online.wsj.com/public/article/SB113474557025824698-3l9 bc8KeTGYeGWhJUm0LLmmn_fQ_20061217.html?mod=tff_main _tff_top.

59. Quoted in Charlie Savage, "Bush Shuns Patriot Act Requirement," *Boston Globe*, March 24, 2006. www.boston.com/news/nation/ar ticles/2006/03/24/bush_shuns_patriot_act_requirement/.

60. Quoted in White House, "President's Statement on H.R. 199, the 'USA PATRIOT Improvement and Reauthorization Act of 2005,'" March 9, 2006. www.whitehouse.gov/news/releases/2006/03/ 20060309-8.html.

61. Quoted in Savage, "Bush Shuns Patriot Act Requirement."

Chapter 5: The Debate Continues

62. Quoted in Lisa Hoppenjans, "Ashcroft Defends Patriot Act: Former Attorney General Questions Critics' Sincerity," *Chapel Hill (NC) News*, September 16, 2006. www.chapelhillnews.com/106/ story/2361.html.

63. Quoted in Preserving Life & Liberty, "Statement of Attorney General Alberto R. Gonzales on the Passage of the USA Patriot Act," March 2, 2006. www.lifeandliberty.gov/.

64. Quoted in Preserving Life & Liberty, "Statement of President George W. Bush on Passage of the Bill to Reauthorize the USA Patriot Act," March 9, 2006. www.lifeandliberty.gov/.

65. Quoted in American Civil Liberties Union, "Despite New Compromise, ACLU Says Patriot Act Debate Far from Over, Pledges to Continue to Work with Bipartisan Allies for Meaningful Changes," February 16, 2006. www.aclu.org/safefree/general/24177prs 20060216.html.

66. American Civil Liberties Union, "The Patriot Act: Where It Stands." http://action.aclu.org/reformthepatriotact/whereitstands.html.

67. *The Uniting and Strengthening America by Providing Appropriate Tools Required to Intercept and Obstruct Terrorism (USA PATRIOT ACT) Act of 2001.*

68. David Cole, "Patriot Act Post-mortem," *Nation*, March 17, 2006. www.agenceglobal.com/article.asp?id=848.

69. Cole, "Patriot Act Post-mortem."

70. Quoted in Dan Eggen, "FBI Sought Data on Thousands in '05," *Washington Post*, May 2, 2006. www.washingtonpost.com/wp-dyn/content/article/2006/05/01/AR200605010138 8.html.

71. Quoted in American Civil Liberties Union, "ACLU Releases First Concrete Evidence of FBI Spying Based Solely on Groups' Anti-War Views," March 14, 2006. www.aclu.org/safefree/spying/ 24528prs20060314.html.

72. Quoted in American Civil Liberties Union, "ACLU Releases First Concrete Evidence of FBI Spying Based Solely on Groups' Anti-War Views."

73. Quoted in Gail Russell Chaddock, "FBI and the USA Patriot Act in the Spotlight as Congress Considers How to Fight Terror," *Christian Science Monitor*, May 3, 2006. www.csmonitor.com/2006/0503/p10s01-uspo.html.

74. Quoted in American Library Association, "FBI Director Questioned on Patriot Act," May 5, 2006. www.ala.org/ala/alonline/current news/newsarchive/2006abc/may2006ab/mueller.htm.

75. American Civil Liberties Union, "The Patriot Act."

76. Quoted in American Civil Liberties Union, "Reauthorized Patriot Act Still Unconstitutional, ACLU Says," August 7, 2006. http://civilliberty.about.com/gi/dynamic/offsite.htm?zi=1/XJ&sdn=civilliberty&zu=http%3A%2F%2Fwww.aclu.org%2Fsafefree%2Fnationalsecurityletters%2F26404prs20060807.html.

77. Quoted in American Civil Liberties Union, "Government Drops Demand for Library Records," June 26, 2006. www.aclu.org/safe free/nationalsecurityletters/index.html/.

78. Quoted in American Civil Liberties Union, "Government Drops Demand for Library Records."

79. *The Uniting and Strengthening America by Providing Appropriate Tools Required to Intercept and Obstruct Terrorism (USA PATRIOT ACT) Act of 2001.*

80. Quoted in PEN American Center, "PEN Praises Ruling in Lawsuit Challenging Visa Denials," June 23, 2006. www.pen.org/viewme dia.php/prmMID/688/prmID/278.

81. Quoted in PEN American Center, "PEN Praises Ruling in Lawsuit Challenging Visa Denials."

82. Bruce Schneier, "Unchecked Presidential Power," *Minneapolis Star Tribune*, December 20, 2005. www.schneier.com/essay-102.html.

83. Elizabeth Drew, "Power Grab," *New York Times Review of Books*, June 22, 2006. www.nybooks.com/articles/19092.

84. Charlie Savage, "Bush Challenges Hundreds of Laws," *Boston Globe*, April 30, 2006. www.boston.com/news/nation/articles/2006/04/30/bush_challenges_hundreds_of_laws/.

85. American Civil Liberties Union, "The Patriot Act."

86. William Kristol and Gary Schmitt, "Vital Presidential Power," *Weekly Standard*, December 20, 2005. www.washingtonpost.com/wp-dyn/content/article/2005/12/19/AR200512190 1027.html.

87. Quoted in Linda Feldmann and Warren Richey, "Power Shift to President May Stick," *Christian Science Monitor*, October 3, 2002. www.csmonitor.com/2002/1003/p01s02-uspo.html.

88. Drew, "Power Grab."

89. Quoted in Scott Shane and Adam Liptak, "Detainee Bill Shifts Power to President," *New York Times*, September 30, 2006. www.nytimes.com/2006/09/30/us/30detain.html?ex=1317268800 &en=a3b420d3ad6008e7&ei=5088&partner=rssnyt&emc=rss.
90. Zogby International, "Voters Balance Privacy, Surveillance," February 2, 2006. www.zogby.com/News/ReadNews.dbm? ID=1068.
91. Quoted in Nat Hentoff, "The War on Privacy," *Village Voice*, February 12, 2006. www.villagevoice.com/news/0607,hentoff,72136,6. html.

Chapter 1: A Response to Terror

1. According to the author, why was the Patriot Act enacted so quickly following the September 11, 2001, terrorist attacks? What was the impact of this quick passage?

2. The stated purpose of the Patriot Act is to deter and punish terrorist acts—how does the act accomplish this goal?

3. Describe the original purpose of the Foreign Intelligence Surveillance Act (FISA) and how this law was affected by the Patriot Act.

Chapter 2: A Controversial Law

1. What were the concerns of librarians who opposed the Patriot Act?

2. Which sections of the Patriot Act have been challenged in court by the American Civil Liberties Union (ACLU), and what did the ACLU argue in these challenges?

3. According to the information provided by the Department of Justice to Congress in May of 2003, how had the Patriot Act been implemented by the government at that point?

Chapter 3: Civil Liberties Versus National Security

1. How did President Bush and his supporters defend the Patriot Act's provisions for searching e-mails, Internet communications, and library computer records?

2. Describe some of the ways that the Patriot Act threatened constitutional rights to privacy, according to civil libertarians.

3. What antiterrorism successes did the Bush administration attribute to the new police powers created by the Patriot Act?

Chapter 4: A Permanent Patriot Act

1. According to the author, why did news reports of domestic spying by the National Security Agency (NSA) delay the reauthorization of the Patriot Act?

2. According to the book, what arguments did Patriot Act opponents advance to contest administration claims that the act had been successful in combating terrorism?

3. Describe some of the safeguards enacted as part of the Patriot Act reauthorization in 2006.

Chapter 5: The Debate Continues

1. According to the author, why are civil libertarians not satisfied with the safeguards in the reauthorized Patriot Act?

2. What evidence of civil rights abuses has surfaced since the Patriot Act's reauthorization in March 2006?

3. In the Patriot Act and other areas, President Bush has sought to expand the power of the president and the executive branch of government to decide how to fight terrorism—do you think this is a good idea? Why or why not?

ORGANIZATIONS TO CONTACT

American Civil Liberties Union (ACLU)
125 Broad St., 18th Floor
New York, NY 10004
(212) 549-2585 • fax: (212) 549-2646
Web site: www.aclu.org

The ACLU is a nonprofit and nonpartisan organization founded in the 1920s, supported by annual dues and contributions from its members, plus grants from private foundations and individuals. The ACLU's mission is to preserve the protections and guarantees contained in the Bill of Rights to the U.S. Constitution, including the First Amendment rights to free speech, association, assembly, and religion; the right to a free press; the right to due process of law; and the right to privacy. The ACLU has been very active in opposing the Patriot Act, and its Web site contains a wealth of information about the act and its implementation.

American Library Association (ALA)
50 E. Huron St.
Chicago, IL 60611
(800) 545-2433
Web site: www.ala.org/ala/pio/mediarelations/patriotactmedia.htm

The ALA is a membership organization founded in 1876 to provide leadership for the development, promotion, and improvement of library and information services and the profession of librarianship in order to enhance learning and ensure access to information for all. The ALA's Web site contains a section on the Patriot Act, explaining its effect on libraries.

Bill of Rights Defense Committee (BORDC)
8 Bridge St., Suite A
Northampton, MA 01060
(413) 582-0110
Web site: www.bordc.org

The BORDC was founded in November 2001 to promote a debate about how the Patriot Act and other antiterrorism legislation affects constitutional civil rights liberties. The groups helped to organize and support a national grassroots movement against the Patriot Act that resulted in anti–Patriot Act resolutions being adopted by eight states and more than four hundred cities and counties. The group's Web site contains a number of helpful links to articles and Internet sites relating not only to the Patriot Act, but also to other legislation and government activities that it perceives as threats to civil liberties.

Center for Constitutional Rights (CCR)

666 Broadway, 7th Floor
New York, NY 10012
(212) 614-6464 • fax: (212) 614-6499
Web site: www.ccr-ny.org/v2/home.asp

The CCR is a nonprofit legal and educational organization dedicated to protecting and advancing the rights guaranteed by the U.S. Constitution and the Universal Declaration of Human Rights. The group uses litigation proactively to defend civil and human rights and has been involved in litigation challenging the Patriot Act. A search on its Web site produces a number of publications relating to the Act.

Center for Democracy and Technology (CDT)

1634 Eye St. NW, #1100
Washington, DC 20006
(202) 637-9800 • fax: (202) 637-0968
Web site: www.cdt.org

The CDT is a nonprofit public policy organization dedicated to promoting a democratic, open, decentralized global Internet. It strives to develop, promote, and implement public policies to preserve and enhance free expression, privacy, open access, and other democratic values in Internet communications. The CDT Web site contains a section on the reauthorized Patriot Act, including legal analyses of its effects on Internet communications.

Electronic Frontier Foundation (EFF)

454 Shotwell St.
San Francisco, CA 94110-1914
(415) 436-9333 • fax: (415) 436-9993
Web site: www.eff.org

The EFF is a donor-funded nonprofit organization founded in 1990 to defend free speech, privacy, innovation, and consumer rights in the Internet and networked world. It fights for these freedoms primarily in the courts, bringing lawsuits against the U.S. government and large corporations. EFF has fought for reforms of the Patriot Act and has filed a lawsuit against AT&T for collaborating with National Security Agency spying. Its Web site contains a section on privacy with information about these issues.

The Heritage Foundation
214 Massachusetts Ave. NE
Washington, DC 20002-4999
(202) 546-4400 • fax: (202) 546-8328
Web site: www.heritage.org/

The Heritage Foundation is a research and educational think tank that seeks to formulate and promote conservative public policies based on the principles of free enterprise, limited government, individual freedom, traditional American values, and a strong national defense. A search of the group's Web site produces numerous articles about the Patriot Act.

U.S. Department of Justice (DOJ)
950 Pennsylvania Ave. NW
Washington, DC 20530-0001
(202) 514-2000
Web site: www.lifeandliberty.gov

The DOJ is the federal agency responsible for enforcing federal laws and conducting investigations and prosecutions of criminal and terrorist activities. This Web site was set up by the department to provide information to the public about the Patriot Act and help win reauthorization of the legislation. It contains information about the reauthorized act, including a text of the law, as well as administration claims about its successes and value as an antiterror tool.

Books

Robert P. Abele, *A User's Guide to the USA PATRIOT Act and Beyond.* Lanham, MD: University Press of America, 2004. An examination of the various provisions in the Patriot Act and other proposed programs and laws that affect privacy, probable cause, due process, and free speech.

John D. Ashcroft, *Never Again: Securing America and Restoring Justice.* New York: Center Street, 2006. A book by former U.S. attorney general John Ashcroft about the challenges presented by the September 11, 2001, terrorist attack, the 2001 Patriot Act, and the nation's war on terrorism.

Howard Ball and Mildred Vasan, *The USA Patriot Act: A Reference Handbook.* Santa Barbara, CA: ABC-CLIO, 2004. An in-depth examination of the balancing of civil liberties against national security, written for young adults.

M. Katherine B. Darmer, Robert M. Baird, and Stuart E. Rosenbaum, eds., *Civil Liberties vs. National Security in a Post-9/11 World.* Amherst, NY: Prometheus, 2004. A collection of articles and opinions written by leading experts on the balance between civil liberties and national security, including a section on the Patriot Act.

Amitai Etzioni, *How Patriotic Is the Patriot Act? Freedom Versus Security in the Age of Terrorism.* New York: Routledge, 2004. A detailed discussion of the original Patriot Act and the balance of national security versus civil liberties in an age of terrorism.

Herbert N. Foerstel, *Refuge of a Scoundrel: The Patriot Act in Libraries.* Westport, CT: Libraries Unlimited, 2004. An overview of the Patriot Act and how its new surveillance powers affect libraries and all Americans, written by a leading library advocate.

Periodicals

Nancy V. Baker, "National Security Versus Civil Liberties," *Presidential Studies Quarterly*, September 2003.

Scott Carlson, "Federal Court Overturns Law-Enforcement Powers Expanded in Patriot Act," *Chronicle of Higher Education*, October 15, 2004.

Nancy Chang, "The USA PATRIOT Act: What's So Patriotic About Trampling on the Bill of Rights?" Center for Constitutional Rights, November 2001. www.ratical.org/ratville/CAH/USAPAanalyze.html.

David Cole, "Patriot Act Post-Mortem," *Nation*, March 17, 2006. www.agenceglobal.com/article.asp?id=848.

Barbara Comstock, "Rhetoric vs. Reality," *National Review Online*, September 3, 2003. www.nationalreview.com/comment/comment-comstock090303.asp.

Congressional Research Service, "Administrative Subpoenas and National Security Letters in Criminal and Intelligence Investigations: A Sketch," April 15, 2005.

————, "USA PATRIOT Act: Background and Comparison of House- and Senate-Approved Reauthorization and Related Legislative Action," August 9, 2005.

Peter Grier, "How the Patriot Act Came In from the Cold," *Christian Science Monitor*, March 3, 2006. www.csmonitor.com/2006/0303/p01s03-uspo.html.

Michael Isikoff, "What the Government Knows," *Newsweek*, June 26, 2006. www.msnbc.msn.com/id/13561813/site/ newsweek/.

Michael Isikoff and Mark Hosenball, "At Work: The Patriot Act," *Newsweek*, July 14, 2004. www.msnbc.msn.com/id/5439022/site/newsweek.

Paul T. Jaeger, Charles R. McClure, John Carlo Bertot, and John T. Snead, "The USA PATRIOT Act," *Library Quarterly*, April 2004.

Alain Leibman, "Good Law, Tough Sell," *New Jersey Law Journal*, July 5, 2004.

Robert O'Harrow Jr., "Six Weeks in Autumn," *Washington Post*, October 27, 2002. www.washingtonpost.com/ac2/wp-dyn?pagename=article&contentId=A1999-2002Oct22&notFound=true.

Web Sites

Civil Liberties Watch: Elaine Cassel: The War at Home, City Pages (http://blogs.citypages.com/ecassel/). A blog by a lawyer and law professor that chronicles the Bush administration's war on terror and its effects on civil liberties, through February 4, 2005.

Life and Liberty, Department of Justice (www.lifeandliberty. gov). A government Web site that provides information about the reauthorized Patriot Act and the government's claims about its successes in the war on terrorism.

National Commission on Terrorist Attacks upon the United States (www.9-11commission.gov/). A government Web site that contains information about the 9/11 Commission's investigation of the September 11, 2001, attacks, including the commission's July 22, 2004, report containing antiterrorism recommendations.

Safe and Free: USA Patriot Act, American Civil Liberties Union (www.aclu.org/safefree/patriot/index.html). This Web site is run by the nation's most well-known civil liberties group and provides information about the group's most recent litigation and other efforts to reform the Patriot Act.

USA Patriot Act and Intellectual Freedom, American Library Association (www.ala.org/ala/oif/ifissues/usapatriotact.htm). A Web site run by the national library association containing information about the Patriot Act, its reauthorization, and the latest news relating to the act.

USA Patriot Act, Electronic Privacy Information Center (www.epic.org/privacy/terrorism/usapatriot/). A Web site run by a civil liberties group that provides a good overview of the Patriot Act and developments through November 2005.

The USA Patriot Act, Public Broadcasting Service (www.pbs.org/newshour/indepth_coverage/terrorism/homeland/patriotact.html). A Web site run by a news service that provides a concise history of the Patriot Act and a summary of its reauthorized provisions.

INDEX

PICTURE CREDITS

Cover: © Bill Varie/CORBIS
AP Images, 12, 15, 21, 29, 30, 34, 38, 43, 48, 50, 54, 55, 57, 60, 62, 64, 72, 76, 78, 80, 81, 85, 87, 89, 90, 93,
Bryan Haraway/Getty Images, 47
Diana Walter/Time & Life Pictures/Getty Images, 19
© George Steinmetz/CORBIS, 7
© Jason Reed/Reuters/CORBIS, 69
Justin Sullivan/Getty Images, 23
Manny Ceneta/Getty Images, 14
Mark Wilson/Getty Images, 9
Matthew Cavanaugh/Getty Images, 35
© Reuters/CORBIS, 18, 66
Steve Zmina, 16, 82
STR/AFP/Getty Images, 27

ABOUT THE AUTHOR

Debra A. Miller is a writer and lawyer with a passion for current events and history. She began her law career in Washington, D.C., where she worked on legislative, policy, and legal matters in government, public interest, and private law firm positions. She now lives with her husband in Encinitas, California. She has written and edited numerous books and anthologies on historical and political topics.